PRESIDENT TRUMP'S PASTOR PAULA WHITE

*The miracle-selling huckster
who became
the spiritual advisor to the
world's most powerful man*

Susan Puzio

President Donald Trump, First Lady Melania Trump, and Paula White

Official White House Photo - Andrea Hanks

Contact the author at

PO Box 3563

Spring Hill, Florida 34611

susan@propheticnews.com

ISBN 978-1-882970-10-0

ISBN (e-book) 978-1-882970-02-5

Library of Congress Control Number: 2022902435
All Scripture references are quoted from the King James
Version of the Bible.
Printed in the United States of America
Cover photo: Official White House photo by White House
photographer Andrea Hanks

Dedication

For all lovers of what is true

"Sanctify them through Thy truth: Thy word is truth." John 17:17

May the next generation of
Reformers
learn from the mistakes of the past.

"Then the king commanded to call the magicians, and the astrologers, and the sorcerers, and the Chaldeans, for to shew the king his dreams. So, they came and stood before the king."

Nebuchadnezzar's Dream, Daniel 2

TABLE of

Contents

Acknowledgements

To my Lord Jesus Christ. He made all things beautiful in His time.

A special thank you to all my friends who helped me with the creation of this book.

Introduction

PSALM 101:3
"I will set no wicked thing before mine eyes:
I hate the work of them that turn aside; it shall not cleave to me. "

Paula White and her husband Jonathan Cain were holding a marriage seminar at her church, the City of Destiny in Apopka, Florida, just outside Orlando.

Families, single adults, children, and teens filled the room that Sunday morning.

Paula giggled. "Wait till we get to your sex life." Jon chimed in, "How freaky do you wanna get? And, ladies, if you don't know what he likes, get a book; go get some porn. If he likes to watch porn, watch PORN with him." Then Jon added, "They even have tapes for couples. You can watch 'em." Paula suggested not to get "addicted to porn" but educate yourself about sexuality.

By being a voyeur?

Never heard that from a pulpit!

(Video link)

https://youtu.be/UMbXrL7q1zU

Chapter One: Who Is Paula White?

Paula Michelle Furr was born April 20, 1966, in Tupelo, a small town in northern Mississippi, which is best known as the birthplace of Elvis Presley.

Her parents were Myra Janelle and Donald Paul Furr III. Donald was killed in 1971 in a car accident at 29. His car went off the road as he was going around a curve at a high speed, and he was thrown from the overturning car, according to published newspaper reports and eyewitness testimony at the scene, a tragic end to a young and promising life.

Paula was only five years old at the time of the accident. (Source: *Northeast Mississippi Daily Journal* April 26, 1971)

Tupelo Man Killed In 1-Car Accident

A Tupelo man was killed instantly in a one-auto accident at 11:45 a.m. Saturday on Highway 78 east of Holly Springs.

Officers said Donald P. Furr III, 29, apparently lost control of his east-bound vehicle on a curve and went off the right side of the highway just outside Holly Springs city limits near Lake Center Restaurant.

Mississippi Highway Patrolman T. K. Clayton, who investigated the accident, said that according to two or three witnesses the 1968 Plymouth "was traveling at an excessive rate of speed and turned over four or five times."

Patrolman Clayton added that Furr, who was dead on arrival at the Marshall County Hospital, was apparently killed instantly having been thrown out of the over-turning car.

Funeral services were held at 5 p.m. Sunday in the Funeral Chapel at W. E. Pegues with burial in Glenwood Cemetery. The Rev. Garland Holloman officiated.

Furr, co-owner of Playland Toy Stores, lived on Ida Street. A graduate of Tupelo High School, he attended the University of Mississippi. He was a member of the First United Methodist Church and a member of the Tupelo Jaycees.

Pallbearers were Ernie Blackwell, Jimmy Riley, Bobby Edwards, David Hervey, Jimmy Coggins, Dan Ballard, Bill McGuire and Jeff Troyka.

He is survived by a daughter, Paula Michelle and one son, David Mark; his parents, Mr. and Mrs. Donald P. Furr Jr.; a sister, Susan Furr; his grandparents, Mr. and Mrs. Donald P. Furr Sr. and Mrs. John Sims, all of Tupelo.

Her mother struggled financially and with alcoholism after her father's premature death. She was a young widow left with two small children and a nightmare memory of a horrific car accident after an argument. A few years later, Myra married Admiral Charles Loar when Paula was nine, so Admiral Loar, who was an accomplished Naval officer and at one time served as commanding officer at Bethesda Naval Hospital (now named Walter Reed), may have acted as a father figure. Thereby, he added emotional and financial stability to the fractured family.

Perhaps it was the loss of her father and her mother's alcoholism that led Paula to exaggerate, manipulate, and stretch the truth, later becoming a gospel huckster and scammer.

Depending on her audience, she sometimes brags about coming from a very wealthy family, yet in her father's and her grandmother's obituaries, there is no mention of the vast business empire Paula claimed that they owned. She made those comments during an interview on the *700 Club* years ago.

I have yet to find one "mansion" she may have lived in as a child, only a photo of one of her childhood homes posted on social media, and it was not a mansion. I did not find any "mansions" her grandmother and grandfather Furr lived in on her father's side either. The homes I found for the Furr family were typically upper-middle-class, nice homes, but not "mansions." Here is a paragraph from her grandmother Furr's obituary:

"Tupelo 10:46 am – Mary Ruth Furr, 93, died Tuesday, April 18, 2017, at Traceway. She was born June 13, 1923, in Guntown to the late John and Anna Barber Sims. She was a longtime and faithful member of the First United Methodist Church of Tupelo. Mary Ruth was the owner and operator of Playland Toy Store and also worked as a sales associate for Reeds Department Store. She also had the great honor of serving as an Ole Miss fraternity house mother. Her spare time was spent with her loving family and playing bridge and golf with friends." (Legacy.com)

It could be possible someone along the way had a large estate. In Paula's autobiography, she says it was her great-grandparents who had wealth.

When Paula was a teenager, she made some of the mistakes many young people do, so when she got pregnant out of wedlock at eighteen, she hastily married Harold Dean Knight, the father of her son, Bradley, who was born in November 1985. However, this marriage was short-lived, especially after Randy White entered the scene.

Paula and Dean legally separated in June 1988 and divorced in October 1989.

Randy was married with three small children, and he was an up-and-coming charismatic evangelist with the Church of God. According to Paula's book, *Something Greater*, they had a sexual affair. (Kindle location 1072)

It was at eighteen when she says she heard the gospel for the first time, and she became a Christian, although her life has been a series of contradictions and hypocrisy. Sometime later, as the story goes, God gave her a vision of shaking nations, whatever that means.

As of this writing, no nations have been shaken, not even the nation of Apopka, as she cannot even grow her congregation there. Thousands have fled her building, and now her membership is in the hundreds, not a mega-church. White Republicans have embraced her in larger numbers because of her association with Donald Trump.

When Dean Knight and Paula divorced, she married Randy White. Moving to Tampa in 1990, Randy eventually became a pastor, and together, they built a large congregation, both serving as senior pastors during the rise and fall of Without Walls International Church.

This marriage lasted about seventeen years. Paula now tells people she never really had a husband until she married Jonathan Cain. Not a good public relations move on her part since Randy could turn on her if given the right opportunity. But maybe he had to sign a non-disclosure agreement as part of his divorce settlement.

During their time in Tampa, the local newspapers took an interest in the fast-growing church and its rapid accumulation of wealth.

The *St. Petersburg Times* and *Tampa Tribune* published many articles about the Whites over the years. In 2008, *Tampa Tribune* reporters Baird Helgeson and Michelle Bearden interviewed family and friends of the Whites and discovered the pastors had their own versions of past events, which did not jive with the accounts from friends.

"When Paula tells her life story, she talks about her childhood and a brief marriage before her marriage to Randy. The story she and Randy have not widely shared involves their time before that at a small church in Damascus, Maryland, when they were married to other people.

"Friends and their relatives who used to attend the church say they have privately boiled as Paula wrote in some books and preached on the air about marrying a rock singer she barely knew and living on 'government cheese.' They insist Paula and her first husband, Dean Knight, were not poor and that the marriage was a loving one on Dean's behalf.

"They said she left him in part because she believed Randy had the charisma and talent to take her far in life. 'What we are bothered by are the hypocrisy and the lies,' said Gretchen Wall, part of a group of teenage friends, including Dean, who grew up together and later embraced Paula." (2008 *Tampa Tribune*)

Paula has conflicting versions of her life story, and here are a few examples.

In her autobiography, *Something Greater*, Paula states that her father could not hold down a job, and "his job was always new." There were also trips to Vegas.

That story is contradicted by another story Paula told on the *700 Club* when she claimed her parents owned toy stores, craft stores, restaurants, and seafood chains. How could they own and operate so many businesses if her dad was squandering "milk" money?

Paula lived in a doublewide mobile home when married to Dean, and at times, she claims they had severe financial hardships. The doublewide was situated on what looks like a nice property in Mt. Airy, Maryland. Hardly the vision she portrays in the sermons of her life in the trailer or of being called trailer trash.

According to court documents from the Shirley Johnson trial, it appears she lent her ex-husband Dean quite a substantial amount of money, over one million dollars, for a business named Center Industries. She even presented him on stage at her church in Apopka. Better be nice to the ex who knows all about your real history before you become the "spiritual advisor" to the president and before the book about your life story comes out.

Photo of Paula's trailer on Bill Moxley Road

Paula White's ex-husband Dean is the registered agent for Center Industries. Why did Paula lend him $1.47 million?

(see next page)

CENTER INDUSTRIES MARYLAND, LLC is a Maryland Domestic LLC filed on November 17, 2016. The company's filing status is listed as Active and its File Number is W17619800.

The Registered Agent on file for this company is Dean Knight

New Destiny Christian Center, Inc. and Subsidiary

Supplementary Consolidating Information
Year Ended December 31, 2017

	New Destiny Christian Center Center Inc.	Paula White Ministries	Center Industries, D.O.O.	Eliminations	Consolidated New Destiny Christian Center Inc.
Assets					
Cash	$ (14,427)	$ 120,190	$ -		$ 105,763
Investments	1,360,041	-	-		1,360,041
Inventories	-	165,190	-		165,190
Notes receivable	-	-	1,470,000		1,470,000
Property and equipment:					
Land and land improvements	4,996,096	-	-		4,996,096
Buildings	6,990,936	-	205,000		7,195,936
Furniture and equipment	447,828	53,053	-		500,881
Vehicles	199,942	-	-		199,942
	12,634,802	53,053	205,000		12,892,855
Less accumulated depreciation	(1,947,557)	(30,779)	-		(1,978,336)
Total property and equipment, net	10,687,245	22,274	205,000	-	10,914,519
Investment in subsidiary	2,000,000	-	-	(2,000,000)	-
Due to Paula White Ministries	290,898	-	-	(290,898)	-
Other assets	22,190	6,000	-		28,190
Total assets	$ 14,345,947	$ 313,654	$ 1,675,000	$ (2,290,898)	$ 14,043,703
Liabilities and Net Assets					
Liabilities:					
Accounts payable and accrued expenses	$ 76,617	$ 155,513	$ -		$ 232,130
Notes payable and lease obligations	1,780,243	888,338	142,000		2,810,581
Due to New Destiny Christian Center, Inc.		290,898	-	(290,898)	-
Due to Paula White Enterprises, Inc.	-	744,368	-		744,368
Total liabilities	1,856,860	2,079,117	142,000	(290,898)	3,787,079
Net assets	12,489,087	(1,765,463)	1,533,000	(2,000,000)	10,256,624
Total liabilities and net assets	$ 14,345,947	$ 313,654	$ 1,675,000	$ (2,290,898)	$ 14,043,703

4

Notice Center Industries

In a June 2010 sermon, she said she was on public assistance when she gave birth to Brad. Yet her stepfather, Admiral Charles Loar, was an accomplished man of means, and by this time, her mother was likely gainfully employed after earning several degrees. Paula said her family did cut her off financially because of Jesus, according to her autobiography, but helping her along the way was a $37,000 inheritance from a trust fund, or was that not true?

Years later, on a TBN broadcast, Paula said she and Randy needed to come up with $600,000 cash in thirty days to buy their now-defunct church building in Tampa. But in a July 22, 2010, sermon, the amount was one million dollars. So, which one is it?

(Source: Paula White False testimony part 2, video YouTube)

https://youtu.be/jky9Gt3NLQo

Her testimony and excerpts of her life story, and there are many different versions, have been documented on the YouTube channel, theremnantsjnj.

Religious media has failed miserably to hold televangelists accountable for their ridiculous methods and fraudulent fundraising techniques. The dangerous prosperity gospel has been exposed by independent researchers who have taken the lead against these corrupt religious leaders.

Shirley Johnson is one of those who captured the important contradictions in Paula's life story.

You can hear and see the video evidence on her channel. All from Paula's mouth. The information compiled by Johnson was the major issue later as Paula sued her for copyright infringement.

In 2018, *The Christian Post* reported:

"A U.S. District Court in Florida has ordered Pastor Paula White to pay $13,707 to a woman for causing 'emotional harm' by suing her for copyright infringement after she posted videos criticizing her church and ministries."

The ruling concerns White's attempt to sue Shirley Johnson for posting videos on YouTube using clips and images from the New Destiny Christian Center and Paula White Ministries to criticize them. The lawsuit was dismissed, and Johnson filed a countersuit for "malicious prosecution," according to Techdirt.com. (Source: Thu., Aug. 2, 2018, 10:46 a.m. — Mike Masnick)

Johnson also filed another lawsuit against White for allegedly deliberately misrepresenting copyright infringement.

Paula had a pattern of legal threats against people who spoke out against her. When you are a public figure, you can expect criticism, and sometimes you can learn from your critics. After all, everyone has blind spots. Paula can hardly blame her critics for repeating words that came out of her mouth, as was the case with Shirley's videos.

Chapter Two: Prosperity Gospel

Much has been said about the "prosperity gospel" when referring to Paula White. For the first fifteen years of my Christian life, I believed that version of the gospel, and I also participated in public ministry.

I witnessed firsthand the greed and materialism that caused me to reject its teachings. After much reflection on the scriptures, I could no longer accept the give-to-get gospel.

If you took a poll in most Evangelical churches, people would have to admit they are still in debt even though they tithe ten percent of their income and do the seed-sowing rituals, which are supposed to help

Christians magically acquire more money from God.

With all the giving the Whites were doing, it did not work for them. This was evident by their huge debts for many years during their time in Tampa.

God does not need money; we do. But the televangelists put their spin on it. God calls money filthy lucre and warns us that the love of it is the ROOT of all evil. We give to each other because, as Christians, we follow God's biblical principle. "For God so loved the world that He gave His only begotten Son." John 3:16. So our giving is an act of love toward others, without selfish motives.

There are no seed-sowing or ten-percent requirements as New Testament believers; all giving is freewill. No one ever approached Jesus when He walked the earth and handed Him money in exchange for prayers or miracles.

In her autobiography, *Something Greater*, Paula is at a loss as to why she is labeled a "prosperity preacher."

"Once I'm on Christian television stations, it is expected for me not only to pay for my airtime but to also participate in telethons. God greatly favors me, and I'm able to raise millions of dollars to help propel the gospel around the world. I do this out of 'purity' and a passion to reach nations with the gospel, not recognizing until much later the false perception and labels it will place on my life and ministry."

White, Paula. *Something Greater* (pp. 110-111). Faith Words. Kindle Edition.

The "false perception" is created by Paula herself, and it is based on reality and the miracle-selling attached to her fundraising techniques. One example was at the "Vision Conference" hosted by the River Church in Tampa; she encouraged people to give their houses and to empty their bank accounts by claiming if God said to do it, then do it. "When God says to lay the keys to your house down at this altar, when God says empty your bank accounts, do it in the name of Jesus." The inference is do it, and God will move for you. Paula has yet to lay her house down or empty her bank accounts of her over $8,000,000 worth of assets.

(about minute 21:40)

https://youtu.be/kqVDcQeOaYA

TV preachers talk about open windows from heaven, but God does not have any money in heaven to give us. Wealth is accumulated by hard work and good financial management, not by giving money to some televangelist who suggests they funnel it to God for our good. It is an age-old con, but it works.

Oral Roberts made millions telling people to use seed-faith. He was the big daddy of this teaching, although when his son, the then Oral Roberts University President Richard Roberts, was pushed out of the university bearing his father's name, they were $50,000,000 in debt. So much for seed-faith. It did not work for them.

The seed-faith teaching is, "Send me (the preacher or anointed one) money as a seed, and God will give it back to you in a greater measure."

I remember one typical Sunday morning many years ago, my former pastor invited a preacher who embraced teachings similar to Paula White's. He preached his sermon, and at the end, he asked people to walk to the front with a $99 seed and to write on their checks what they were believing God for.

Was it finances you needed? Were you single, and were you believing God for marriage? Or did you need healing in your body?

I sat in the front row when an elderly lady who could barely walk made her way to the front, waving her check eagerly, believing that was the way to get her miracle. How could the church leaders look at her desperation and accept her check?

Telling people God's blessings are free for the asking is not acceptable to the greedy prosperity preachers. They use Mafia-like techniques to try to silence you. There is big money to be made, so don't interfere.

Why would anyone want to earn a living using such despicable tactics? I ask Paula White that question. Why would a woman who has been given so much continue to abuse her position by miracle selling?

A November 2019 *Newsweek* article perfectly pinpoints the problem with White's ministry:

"Richard W. Painter, who served as the chief ethics lawyer in President George W. Bush's White House, blasted President Donald Trump's personal spiritual adviser Paula White, suggesting the religious leader was committing 'fraud' and running a 'Ponzi scheme.'"

BY JASON LEMON ON 11/13/19 AT 10:55 AM EST

The White House recently announced that White, who previously served as the senior pastor of New Destiny Christian Center in Florida, would officially spearhead Trump's Faith and Opportunity Initiative.

Since taking on the official role, the prominent televangelist has continued to sell religious items she claims will provide spiritual and material benefits to buyers. "This 'prosperity gospel' scam by Paula White tests the boundaries between 'religious freedom' and criminal mail fraud and wire fraud," Painter argued in a Wednesday morning tweet. "'Send me money and God will make you rich.' Now she uses her White House position to make her sales pitch." (*Newsweek* 11/18/2019)

Why did President Trump put Paula White in a position of influence in his administration when there are many other qualified men and women with integrity who could serve?

I have never heard President Trump say that Paula White is his pastor, but I have heard Paula say he calls her that. I don't doubt he may have said that to her even though he has made no public declaration about where he goes to church or who his pastor is or if he indeed is born again.

While the book *Something Greater*, her autobiography, provides a public relations version of Paula White's story, her sermons, and television appearances fill in key details left out of the book, especially concerning the prosperity gospel. Most of that information has already been made available on the internet, and once it is posted, it does not disappear. She can deny all day long she is not a prosperity preacher, but the evidence says otherwise.

Chapter Three: Ministry Integrity

Any person who puts themselves out there as a born-again Christian in ministry is held to a higher standard, and it comes with much public scrutiny, as it should. The Bible clearly says we should be held to that higher standard, especially since we believe one's eternal destiny could be at stake.

When candidate Trump appeared at a rally in Tampa, Florida, in 2016, I decided to attend. I wanted to see what it would be like to see him in person and to feel the excitement of the crowd.

Paula White was announced, and I said to myself, "What in the world is she doing here?" This was the woman who told people to send her one month's salary, or if you wanted a baby, you could also give a financial offering. Make your checks out to Paula, and she will get it to God for you.

Paula and ex-husband Randy White blew through over one hundred million dollars, and in the end, the "ministry" went bankrupt. I was astonished.

When she approached the front of the stage, I let out a few boos and a security guard swiftly appeared in front of me, telling me I could not boo. No freedom of speech at this Trump rally.

Why would I want to boo Paula? Because she is someone who seems disingenuous about her commitment to Christ. The fundraising techniques she employs are not biblical, and they are meant to deceive the wounded sheep whom God loves. This is contemptible behavior for any "Christian" leader.

So, how did Paula wind up in the White House?

Chapter Four: Meeting Donald Trump

This is the story Paula tells about meeting Mr. Trump. Donald Trump called her after seeing her on TV at his Mar-a-Lago estate in Palm Beach, Florida. The gorgeous home was built by Marjorie Merriweather Post, yes, the heir to the Post fortune and at one time the richest woman in America.

They struck up a friendship that has since lasted over twenty-four years, with her spending time at his New York offices, and according to her, he even wanted to build a cathedral with her serving as the pastor.

It has been reported that Mr. Trump has an incredible intellect. After spending time with Paula White, I can hardly believe that he concluded she had amazing spiritual or political acumen or exceptional brilliance to share with him, or was he only using her to help secure the Evangelical vote?

She may have seemed like a willing patsy, with enough pride and the feeling of her own self-importance, often referring to herself as an Esther of biblical fame. Trump is a powerful man, and he could encourage her and her delusions of grandeur by helping him sway Christians to vote for him.

Paula White was accepted by certain groups because other social climbers wanted access to Trump. She was hanging by a thread in Evangelical circles, basically washed up until Donald Trump put her back on the map.

This appears as a foreshadowing of the anti-Christ and the false prophet. I am not saying Donald Trump is an anti-Christ figure, but the anti-Christ will promote the false prophet, who will look and sound like a real Christian. Although we may agree with the policies of certain politicians, we must always be looking for fruit that coincides with one's actions.

Christians may now feel betrayed by Mr. Trump, especially where the pro-life movement is concerned. We were led to believe he was the most pro-life President. The evidence proves otherwise.

The use of the tissue from aborted babies for research continued under his administration. Some of the vaccines he promoted were tested and some were developed using the cells from aborted children. You can find this information on the manufacturer's websites, although all vaccine manufacturers deny the cells made it into the final product.

(From the Johnson and Johnson website)

"Johnson & Johnson Announces a Lead Vaccine Candidate for COVID-19; Landmark New Partnership with U.S. Department of Health & Human Services; and Commitment to Supply One Billion Vaccines Worldwide for Emergency Pandemic Use | Johnson & Johnson (jnj.com)

"For more than 20 years, Johnson & Johnson has invested billions of dollars in antivirals and vaccine capabilities. The COVID-19 vaccine program is leveraging Janssen's proven AdVac® and PER.C6® technologies that provide the ability to rapidly develop new vaccine candidates and upscale production of the optimal vaccine candidate. The same technology was used to develop and manufacture the Company's Ebola vaccine and construct our Zika, RSV, and HIV vaccine candidates which are in Phase 2 or Phase 3 clinical development stages.

"The fetal cell lines being used to test or manufacture the COVID-19 vaccines are from two sources: ● HEK-293: A kidney cell line that was isolated from a fetus in 1973 (undisclosed origin, from either a spontaneous miscarriage or an elective abortion) ● PER.C6: A retinal cell line that was isolated from an aborted fetus in 1985."

(source:COVID19_Vaccine_Fetal_Cell_Handout.pdf

The University of Pittsburgh performed gruesome experiments partially funded by our National Institute of Allergy and Infectious Diseases (NIAID) with Anthony Fauci at the helm. Did Fauci know? Then-President Trump stood alongside Fauci on many occasions as they prepared to roll out the vaccines. Was he that ignorant of what was going on at the NIH? I make no excuses for him here. They used the scalps from aborted children on the heads of mice in a taxpayer-funded grant. How did all of the pro-life Trump advisors miss this one?

Printed in the *Sun* newspaper, a British publication by Patrick Know, July 28, 2021:

Dr. Fauci's agency funded Frankenstein research that saw aborted babies' body parts grafted to MICE to grow hair and organs (the-sun.com)

Newsweek also reported on this May 26, 2021, David Daleiden:

University of Pittsburgh Won't Explain its Planned Parenthood Ties | Opinion (newsweek.com)

Here is an excerpt from that story:

"In one study published last year, Pitt scientists described scalping 5-month-old aborted babies to stitch onto the backs of lab rats. They wrote about how they cut the scalps from the heads and backs of the babies, scraping off the 'excess fat' under the baby's skin before stitching it onto the rats. They even included photos of the babies' hair growing out of the scalps. Each scalp belonged to a little Pennsylvania baby whose head would grow those same hairs if he or she were not aborted for experiments with lab rats."

Another big red flag is Francis Collins, who served as the National Institutes of

Health director during both the Obama and Trump administrations. He claims to be a Christian, yet aborted baby cell lines were used for experimentation purposes under his direction.

Here is a very alarming quote from an interview he gave to Maina Mwaura, CP Guest Contributor. It was posted on the "Christian" Post website.

"He believes people should 'recognize, after all, that people have elective terminations of pregnancy every day, and those materials are being discarded.

"'Suppose it was possible on a rare instance for something that's about to be discarded with full consent after the decision by the mother to be used to develop something that might save somebody's life,' the 71-year-old geneticist reasoned.

" 'In that case, I think even God could look at that and go, "OK, it's not the thing that I would have wanted to see happening. Still, as an ethical choice between discarding or using for some benevolent purpose, maybe that's defensible." Now that will make some people uneasy.' "

Quite a shocking statement to infer that God the Creator and Lover of all life would endorse the use of cells from murdered children to further scientific research.

So, it was not only the likes of Paula White surrounding the president but a motley crew of other men and women who did evil in the sight of the Lord.

After the phone call from Mr. Trump, she cultivated their relationship in part by attending etiquette classes, which baffles me because she was more concerned about behaving properly before Donald Trump than before the Lord Jesus Christ. (quote from *Something Greater*)

"When I get off the line, I am energized and encouraged by the unexpected phone call.

"God's using Paula White Ministries to bless someone like Donald Trump. I smile, knowing God always has a plan.... I believe good things are to come with our thriving ministry. 'I need you to set me up etiquette lessons,' I tell my assistant one day not long after talking to Trump. She smiles and asks me why. 'Because God is preparing me for places.'"

White-Cain, Paula. *Something Greater* (Kindle Locations 2552-2554). Faith Words. Kindle Edition

She appeared on a Facebook live broadcast the day her book, *Something*

Greater, was released, October 15, 2019, and she declared, "They say I am a heretic." So, how did she get from little ole Tupelo to making national headlines as a "heretic"?

After Paula appeared on the *Jim Bakker Show* in October 2019 to promote her book about how God helped her throughout her life, a Mother Jones reporter said Paula mentioned Trump more than she mentioned God in her autobiography.

She just cannot seem to understand the skepticism as she lamented to God, "What did I do wrong?" God supposedly said to her, "Maybe you didn't do something wrong; you did something right," as she proceeded to fleece the people:

"Right now, someone is about to send you that million-dollar check, in the name of Jesus," White said. "You just simply need to be obedient, whether it's $100,000, whether it's $10,000 ... You have got to right now become one of those pillars, become one of those people, whether it's the $10,000 or the $1,000 — and with all due respect, as great as that name is gonna be left there, there's a greater name that's gonna be written.

"Every treasure you give here on earth is being stored up in Heaven. There is a Department of Treasury up in Heaven ... God is watching over everything you do, and you are storing up eternal treasure that will go so far beyond, I think, that we could even begin to imagine."

Jim Bakker is a well-known TV evangelist who once took in over $100,000,000 a year and authored *I Was Wrong*, but now he seems to have changed his testimony about how God had to put him in federal prison for five years to straighten him out.

He brought Paula on his broadcast and flattered her incessantly, calling her the greatest female preacher he ever heard. Paula returned the flattery by asking people to sow large financial seeds, even taking out her checkbook to be the first one to donate a thousand dollars.

Jim Bakker shot to fame, along with his ex-wife Tammy Faye, and they founded the PTL television network and built a vast empire, including a Christian theme park.

In 1989, he was convicted of fraud and served five years in prison. He denies the fraud charges to this day but admits to his affair or one-night stand with Jessica Hahn that led to his downfall. It was quite the scandal. So, it seems Jim would stay far away from characters like Paula, but that easy money could have been the lure, along with invitations to the White House.

By not taking note of the Lord Jesus' playbook, Paula has yet to come clean or repent of her Tetzel-like tactics as she purports to stand for Jesus Christ. Johann Tetzel, a Catholic monk, sold indulgences or time out of Purgatory (a Catholic place of cleansing before you can go on to Heaven), which helped to build St. Peter's Basilica in the fifteenth century.

Paula somehow winds up as the "spiritual advisor" to the president, and I am saying to myself, "Why is the press not reporting on the real Paula White? It cannot be true that she is advising the president about spiritual matters." I cannot believe it, and I wasn't the only one saying that.

Since then, news outlets have been reporting about Paula White as she has become more visible to the general public because of her relationship with President Trump. Because of that, the news media has been watching her ministry services, and it is harder for her to take back what is on audio, video, and what she has written.

Her so-called "ministry" career is filled with serving another Jesus whom many Christians do not recognize. Her Jesus asks for money to do miracles. The love she talks about is shallow and self-serving. She pulls out the verses that will meet her needs. Her Jesus is a god you must pay off by sending her money so he can do things for you. Her Jesus is a pale comparison to the real Jesus.

She exploits the needs and wounds of the gullible who are desperate for God's intervention.

Paula often reminds her audience of the Old Testament command: "Do not come before me empty-handed." However, she fails to point out that Christians are not required to observe the Old Testament feasts because Jesus fulfilled the law. He is our Passover Lamb.

JOHN 1:29

"The next day John seeth Jesus coming unto him, and saith, Behold the Lamb of God, which taketh away the sin of the world."

Also, during His earthly ministry, Jesus never asked for Passover offerings or Day of Atonement offerings.

Such is the life of Paula White. Her belief in the "law of reciprocity" requires no faith or trust in God for finances, and the Bible says whatever is not of faith is sin.

As she masquerades as a saved person, her fruit and actions tell another story. The Bible does say we will know who the true followers of Jesus are by their fruit.

Christians can and do sin. Godly sorrow is evidence of a changed heart, but in this instance after thirty-plus years in public "ministry," her life does not reflect the character of Jesus, the One who gave His life for us. It is another Jesus and another gospel.

Presidential "spiritual advisors" come and go. Psychic Jeanne Dixon met with Nixon and advised Nancy Reagan.

Astrologer Joan Quigley met with the Reagans regularly, although Nancy seems to be the one who was enamored with her.

They are quickly forgotten after the presidential term ends.

Paula's role as a presidential advisor will soon be forgotten, but she will be remembered for telling people not to pay their bills, to tithe first to the church, or else be cursed as *Newsweek* reported on February 18, 2020.

"Then what I'm saying is, FPL (Florida Power and Light) I just made you chief. I just made you fundamental. I just made you the basis to support all structure. So, FPL, heal my child. Find my children that are lost. FPL, open the door for me to get a promotion. FPL, I serve you. I honor you to redeem off of me the curse that is upon all mankind. Because you have just made FPL the first - because you gave the first $100 to pay your electric bill.

"You can't just bring a gratitude offering. It has to be a First Fruits offering! If it is one week's salary if it is a month. If it's a day, it's got to be the whole of something.

"Instead of writing [that check] to the house of God as I'm instructed to, then what I'm saying spiritually is, FPL, I have now established a spiritual law that put you first. So, FPL, save my family, FPL, deliver my drug-addicted son. FPL, kill this cancer that doctors say is in my body."

Or who can forget the satanic pregnancy debacle:

https://youtu.be/TR_slS9qxQs

"I command all satanic pregnancies to miscarry right now. We declare that anything that's been conceived in satanic wombs, that it will miscarry, it will not be able to carry forth any plan of destruction, any plan of harm."

(https://time.com/5771920/trump-paula-white-miscarriage-satanic-pregnancies/)

Soon after this, the coronavirus hit with a vengeance. So much for her empty declarations.

Or how about her alleged recent visit to Heaven where she says she visited the actual throne room of God:

"I literally went to the Throne Room of God, there was a mist that was coming off the water, and I went to the throne of God, and I didn't see God's face clearly, but I saw the face of God ... I knew it was the face of God.

"He put a mantle [on me] and it was a very distinct mantle. There was a mantle, and I saw it very distinctly, the color was like a goldish, a yellowish goldish ... and then I saw the Earth for a moment, and [God] brought me back, and he put me in certain places, one being the White House, one being certain continents.

"I didn't come out of that really until the next day." (Paula White sermon, February 2020 King Jesus Ministry) https://youtu.be/k2UHhKr5oPM

The Bible says no one has seen God and lived; Paula again is spinning her version of the Bible.

E X O D U S 3 3: 2 0

"And he said, Thou canst not see my face: for there shall no man see me, and live."

Trump recently appeared in a video shown at Paula White's church for Pastor Appreciation Day in December 2021. Even though she receives over one million dollars a year in salary and benefits, she needed another appreciation offering and a birthday gift. (about minute 46)

https://youtu.be/2EKomipyxrI

Trump encouraged the poor souls to give Paula money and said he would be working with Paula and has continued to collaborate with her as she now serves as Chair for the Center for American Values at AFPI or America First Policy Institute. Don't laugh. I know it is hard to contain oneself when a person who has no values chairs the Center for American Values. Remember she was the one who giggled when her husband told her congregation to watch porn.

References: for vaccine information (for information purposes only, some are Catholic websites, and I am not endorsing Catholicism)

VaccineDevelopment_FetalCellLines.pdf (lacounty.gov)

Fetal Cell Lines Were Used to Make the Johnson & Johnson COVID Vaccine—Here's What That Means (msn.com)

Quote from the website Children of God for life:

Aborted Fetal Cell Lines

"When we say that vaccines are produced or tested using aborted fetal cell lines, we are referring to a lineage of cells that originated with the corpse of an aborted child. Cells are taken from the child's body and if these cells will multiply indefinitely, then cell lines can be grown. Researchers use these cells to grow viruses for vaccines, or they use the cell lines to test if a vaccine will work. The cells simulate how the human body will respond since they are human cells. They are, however, all the same, so testing and production can be carried out in a predictable environment. Here we provide proof that these cell lines come from abortion."

Vaccine Overview | Children of God for Life (cogforlife.org)
What you need to know about the COVID-19 vaccines - Charlotte Lozier Institute
PER.C6 Cell Lines - Creative Biolabs (gmp-creativebiolabs.com)

Where does PER c6 come from?

Created from retinal tissue of 18-week gestation aborted fetus. Developed in

1985, **PER C6** is the growth medium for a wide variety of human disease-causing viruses that can be processed into inactivated whole virus, live-attenuated, live-vector, split, subunit, and recombinant vaccines.

Microsoft PowerPoint – RD Vaccine platforms Blueprint Janssen_Jenner_21July2016 FINAL mod 22AUG16 (who.int)

I am not anti-vax. I am for ethical vaccines and freedom of choice.

Chapter Five: Paula White Bows to the Cult Leader, Mrs. Moon of the Moonies

During some of Paula White's public appearances, she proudly declares that the reason she has achieved so much in her life is because she is not for sale. In other words, she did not sell herself out by abusing the gospel of Jesus Christ for her monetary gain.

But that could not be further from the truth if anyone has ever heard her hawking the gospel for a price and also praising cult leaders as a paid speaker. She is truly deceived.

Other individuals from the past have gone down a dark road, demanding that people call them mother or father. Hak Ja Han Moon, or Mother Moon, refers to herself as "True Parent" or "True Mother." Orthodox Christianity follows the biblical directive to call no man father (or mother), for we have one Father in Heaven.

Matthew 23:9
"And call no *man* your father upon the earth: for one is your Father, which is in heaven."

Paula White has for the last few years been a featured speaker at conferences for the cult leader, Mother Moon. In December 2021 in South Korea, Paula said Mrs. Moon "loves the Lord," although she (Moon) thinks that she is the Holy Spirit and the literal bride of Christ.

(Quote from *the Journal of Unification Studies* Volume XVII - (2016))

"To add to all that has been said, there is another way to look at True Mother that reveals the nature and scope of her mission after Rev. Moon's passing, when she would be working independently of him. That is to view her in light of her role as the substantial Holy Spirit.

"That identity and role means that True Mother comes in the flesh to do what the Holy Spirit has done in the spirit. The Holy Spirit was most active in the church after Pentecost when Jesus had already ascended to heaven. Therefore, it behooves us in these days after True Father has ascended to heaven, to look again at the role of the Holy Spirit in the days of the primitive church and compare it to the work of True Mother in the present day."

Again, in a speech from 1959, shortly before the Holy Wedding in 1960, Rev. Moon used biblical language to describe how his bride-to-be, the woman who would become True Mother, would come as the substantial Holy Spirit, "the Holy Spirit... in the flesh":

Paula's spiritual deception is remarkable. How can you believe Jesus Christ is the only begotten Son, yet you appear and flatter someone as deceived as Mrs. Sun Myung Moon?

"Many thousands of people participated in activities around and during the 2017 Madison Square Garden event, which was organized by the Family Federation for World Peace and Unification. The keynote remarks by Dr. Hak Ja Han Moon, who founded the organization with her late husband, Rev. Dr. Sun Myung Moon, set a precedent for each rally on five continents.

"Pastor Paula White-Cain took the stage and reminded the audience, 'We're not waiting for change; we bring change.'" (*The Washington Times*. Special Sections Department - Thursday, August 23, 2018)

In her speeches, Mrs. Moon refers to herself as the "*Only Begotten Daughter*" at least 180 times. Theologically, it means "The first one born without sin and begotten from God." Only one who is born without sin could reach Perfection...for anyone else is easy prey for Satan.

However, Jesus Christ is the only begotten Son of God.

"For God so loved the world, that he gave his only begotten Son, that whoever believeth in him should not perish, but have everlasting life." John 3:16

Mrs. Moon believes she is the literal bride of Jesus:

"Jesus having said that he would host the marriage supper of the Lamb indicates that he would not come again in the spirit. He needed to come again in a physical body. I can talk a long time about this, but in short, for the first time in six thousand years, Heaven brought his only daughter to be born through the Korean people. The only son and daughter, who had fulfilled their responsibilities wed and became the True Parents."

In December 2021, Paula bowed to Mother Moon at a conference in South Korea and accepted money and other perks from the Unification Church.

https://youtu.be/2Jh3wz_v2bg

Mrs. Moon declares that she and only she is the only begotten daughter of God, and she repeated this at her Peace Rally where Paula was the featured speaker. Mrs. Moon also declares that her husband was the Messiah and that Jesus Christ was a failure.

Paula, the ever-cunning deceiver, told her congregation she was going to South Korea but failed to mention whom she was going to meet with. Paula bragged about the importance of taking this trip, and the lost sheep at her "church" bought it. She returned to South Korea in February 2022 to speak at a conference where Donald Trump, Mike Pence, Newt Gingrich, and his wife and Mike Pompeo all gave speeches, praising Moon as the "Mother of Peace." Will Paula ever tell her congregation the truth about her association with Moon? Most likely not.

In December 2021, while Paula White was speaking for the wife of deceased cult leader, Sun Myung Moon, they introduced her as the pastor of a mega-church of over 20,000 members. On the day I visited in 2018, there were maybe 400 to 500 people in attendance in a church that once boasted thousands of members. Paula needs to correct her bio.

Mr. Trump also appeared via video for Mrs. Moon on several occasions, another reason Evangelicals should avoid Trump as our choice for president. One was at the Rally for Hope. Trump said it was a profound honor as he praised Moon and said she was a tremendous person. He credited Paula White for his participation in the event. That was pretty low!

Mike Pence, Mike Pompeo, and Jonathan Falwell also all appeared via video for Moon at other rallies, not just in 2022. I guess the money she pays them is too good to pass up. A total betrayal. No real Christian would sing the praises of this evil woman or be caught dead sharing a platform with her.

Video link to the Trump appearance
https://youtu.be/B2ecGNx4294

Paula bows to the cult leader who says she is God.

Who is
True Mother?
10 Aspects to her identity

1. The Only-Begotten Daughter
2. The Mother of Salvation
3. The Mother of Victory
4. The Mother of Cheon Il Guk
5. The Mother of peace
6. The Mother of Unification
7. The Mother of Love and Reverence
8. The Mother of Comfort
9. The Mother of Blessings
10. The Mother of Achievement

Quote from Paula White's speech at the Moon conference, December 2021:
"I want to honor and encourage Mother Moon for her great work as a spiritual leader. Who loves the Lord deeply and she seeks to carry out and give comfort to God's heart."

Dr. Hak Ja Han Moon

Host, Rally of Hope
Co-Founder,
Universal Peace
Federation

H.E. Hun Sen

Prime Minister
Kingdom of Cambodia

**H.E. José Manuel
Barroso**

President
European Commission
(2004-2014)

Hon. Donald Trump

President
United States of
America
(2017-2021)

H.E. H.D. Deve Gowda

**H.E. Gloria Macapagal
Arroyo**

H.E. Nataša Mićić

**H.E. Anthony Thomas
Aquinas Carmona**

2 John 1:7

"For many deceivers are entered into the world, who confess not that Jesus Christ is come in the flesh. This is a deceiver and an antichrist."

Think Tank 2022 Forum

Keynote Speaker

"While the reunification of their homeland has been a cherished dream of all Koreans, we must understand that the dream of reunification will only be achieved by an unwavering commitment of freedom, security and peace."

—Hon. Mike Pence, U.S. Vice President (2017-2021)

Follow this link for the shocking beliefs of the Moonies on their website (for information purposes only):

The Words of Hak Ja Han (Mrs. Sun Myung Moon) before 2013 - TOC (tparents.org)

Biblical Proofs That Jesus Should Have Married (Volume XX – (2019))

"'...the bride of Christ' in the New Testament." [94] Ultimately, the bride must be a substantial person. In order to solve the sinful lineage originated at the fall of our first human ancestors, a physical. (*Journal of Unification Studies* Vol. 20, 2019 - Pages 163 – 195, by Robert Kittel)

For mainstream Unificationists, [1] it is an article of faith that Hak Ja Han Moon (known by the title "True Mother") the widow of the late Rev. Sun Myung Moon (known by the title "True Father"), is entitled to lead the Unification movement. The main reason adduced for this is because together they occupy the position of True Parents, the perfected original point of creation. Theologically speaking, they, as a couple, are the embodiment of <u>God</u> united in His masculinity and Her femininity; hence from the perspective of the Principle of Creation, the True Parents are one, and eternally so.

Definition of a cult: "separate religious group generally claiming compatibility with Christianity but whose doctrines contradict those of historic Christianity and whose practices and ethical standards violate those of biblical Christianity."

As a side note, the *Washington Post* on July 12, 2023, reported Trump was paid at least $2,000,000 to speak for Mrs. Moon.

Chapter Six: Jonathan Cain Meets Paula White

Jonathan Cain met Paula on an airplane in 2011 (or so he says) while he was still married to his beautiful wife Liz. Together, they raised three children and enjoyed a prosperous lifestyle.

Paula and Jon say that God put them together on this flight, but God is not a homewrecker. God does not hook people up when the woman is single, and the man is married, and it later leads to a marriage after he divorces his wife.

Supposedly, they stayed in touch and got together in 2014, but that sounds like Christian spin, or perhaps his autobiography was a work of fiction when he talks about his relationship with Paula.

Paula did buy a condominium in Nashville in 2013, so they were in close "touch." His family home was in Brentwood, outside of Nashville at the time. Jon said his divorce was pending and according to Jon's autobiography, *Don't Stop Believin'*, the couple enjoyed "smoldering kisses" at his golf tournament in California.

Another odd statement about the character of Paula White: what single woman of God shares smoldering kisses with a married man?

I would love to hear Liz's side of the story. How did she feel about Paula "ministering" to her husband before their divorce? Paula said in her 2020 Easter sermon that God accused her of stealing.

She said she always tried to steal love, so would she then try to steal other people's boyfriends? And husbands?

I have no idea what went on behind closed doors between Jon and Liz, but Jon's admitted adultery with other women during his marriage to her may have caused a wound that was hard to heal.

(Excerpt from *Don't Stop Believin'*)

"After separating from Liz and moving into the studio apartment, I was playing in a golf tournament in Pebble Beach. I had emailed Paula to let her know about my pending divorce and Weston's rehab progress. (as if she didn't know)

"I couldn't help but wonder what it would be like to be together in such a romantic setting with a woman I shared my life story with on the plane years ago. With a woman who shared her own life story freely and gave me hope about my faith being restored. We had kept in touch, but now I jokingly mentioned that I wanted to fly her out to join me. (What about those trips to Nashville?)

"To my surprise, she accepted my offer. We spent three days in deep conversation about healing, restoration, and commitment. There were walks along the ocean and kisses that lingered and smoldered like I hadn't felt since I was a teen."

Cain, Jonathan. *Don't Stop Believin'* p. 288. Zondervan. Kindle Edition

Odd that they talked about commitment, but the ink was not yet dry on his divorce papers.

Oh, he was so surprised that she accepted as if they had not spent some cozy times in Nashville before the divorce filing. I would love to talk to the doorman of that building if there is one! Kisses that lingered with someone else's husband!

Jonathan Cain, very early in their relationship, sat on the stage through a Paula White birthday celebration at New Destiny in Apopka with what looked like a straight face as grown men or PITs (pastors in training) under "apostle" Paula called her "Mother" and some even cried as they spoke of their love for her.

She was "incubating" them for future ministry as was the testimony of one pitiful pastor in training, and he even called her "divine."

https://youtu.be/jf221RbcrDo

Chapter Seven: Did Paula White Lie About Her Marriages to Jonathan Cain?

In the video "You love that booty," a sermon Paula White preached at Without Walls years ago, she said, "By eight years old, I could seduce a grown man, have sex with him, and connect with him..." That comment came from a woman who had been sexually abused as a child.

https://youtu.be/OW2gc3Kgg_4

So, was it seduction or coincidence that two of her husbands were married when she met them, and both divorced their wives and married Paula, including her current husband, Jonathan Cain, who achieved fame as a member of the rock band Journey?

Cain paid out millions to his ex-wife Liz in the divorce settlement, which was finalized in October 2014. He claimed he married Paula White for the first time in December 2014 in Ghana, Africa, then again in April 2015 in Apopka, Florida, although that marriage appears to have been staged, because there was no marriage certificate or license issued in that county for that year. The official marriage took place in February 2016. The marriage certificate was recorded at the courthouse in Orange County, Florida.

They had an elaborate "wedding" in April 2015. Paula wore a custom-made wedding gown, and she was "married" by Doug Shackleford, her then-associate pastor, in an outdoor extravaganza, complete with doves and a special song Jon wrote for his bride. It was quite the production, although they never got a license for that "marriage."

Jon lived in Brentwood, Tennessee, with his ex-wife Liz before he married Paula. Brentwood is near Nashville, where Jon has a recording studio, Addiction Sound, and where, in 2013, Paula purchased a condominium. Her purchase there was likely to be near the then-married Jon. According to the divorce documents, Jon and Liz separated in February 2014. Isn't it odd that "pastors" are the ones who help restore marriages, but not when it is "Pastor Paula"?

Paula White and Jonathan Cain announced in December 2014 on the stage of her church that they got married on December 6 in Ghana, Africa, by one

Duncan Williams. Paula calls him "Papa," and he is also referred to as Archbishop Nicolas Duncan Williams. Duncan also uses the prosperity gospel methods similar to Paula's to fund his lifestyle and "ministry." He dresses like a Catholic priest, Roman collar, and all the priestly garb that is associated with religious foolishness.

They have lived together as husband and wife since that time. In a tax filing by Paula for 2014 and 2015, she filed as single. According to the IRS, a married person cannot file as single unless separated or divorced.

Two-Year Comparison Worksheet

2014

Name(s) as shown on return			Social security number
PAULA M. WHITE			▮-6232

2013 Filing Status SINGLE		2014 Filing Status SINGLE	
2013 Tax Bracket 0.0%		2014 Tax Bracket 39.6%	

Description	Tax Year 2013	Tax Year 2014	Increase (Decrease)
WAGES, SALARIES, AND TIPS	513,410.	646,211.	132,801.
SCHEDULE B - TAXABLE INTEREST	949.	843.	-106.
SCHEDULE B - ORDINARY DIVIDENDS	13,422.	19,479.	6,057.
SCHEDULE B - QUALIFIED DIVIDENDS	13,079.	18,721.	5,642.
SCHEDULE D (CAPITAL GAIN/LOSS)	-3,000.	-3,000.	
FORM 4797 (OTHER GAINS OR LOSSES)	-453,261.	0.	453,261.
SCHEDULE E (RENTAL AND PASSTHROUGH)	-113,975.	107,630.	221,605.
OTHER INCOME	400.	-69,720.	-70,120.
TOTAL INCOME	-42,055.	701,443.	743,498.

wo-Year Comparison Worksheet			201!
sme(s) as shown on return 'AULA M. WHITE			Social security number ***-**-623
)14 Filing Status SINGLE		2015 Filing Status SINGLE	
)14 Tax Bracket 39.6%		2015 Tax Bracket 39.6%	
Description	Tax Year 2014	Tax Year 2015	Increase (Decrease)
AGES, SALARIES, AND TIPS	646,211.	748,498.	102,287
CHEDULE B - TAXABLE INTEREST	843.	798.	-45
CHEDULE B - ORDINARY DIVIDENDS	19,479.	16,793.	-2,686
CHEDULE B - QUALIFIED DIVIDENDS	18,721.	16,389.	-2,332
CHEDULE D (CAPITAL GAIN/LOSS)	-3,000.	-3,000.	
CHEDULE E (RENTAL AND PASSTHROUGH)	107,630.	56,195.	-51,435
THER INCOME	-69,720.	1.	69,721
TOTAL INCOME	701,443.	819,285.	117,842

Paula's tax filing for 2015, financial documents were made public and unsealed by the Orlando court after the Shirley Johnson trial. Paula filed as single, although she claimed to be "married."

WARRANTY DEED

BILL GARRETT, Davidson County

Trans: T20130088856 DEEDWARR

Recvd: 10/15/13 13:35 2 pgs
Fees:13.00 Taxes:1295.00

20131015-0107742

G-RR-13-239-502

STATE OF Tennessee

COUNTY OF Davidson

THE ACTUAL CONSIDERATION OR VALUE, WHICHEVER IS GREATER, FOR THIS TRANSFER IS $350,000.00

_____ Affiant

Subscribed and sworn to before me, this 10th DAY OF October, 2013.

_____ Notary Public

MY COMMISSION EXPIRES: 1-9-16

(AFFIX SEAL)

MEGAN PAULUS
STATE OF TENNESSEE
NOTARY PUBLIC
DAVIDSON COUNTY

THIS INSTRUMENT WAS PREPARED BY

Rudy Title & Escrow, LLC
2012 21st Avenue South
Nashville, TN 37212

ADDRESS NEW OWNER(S) AS FOLLOWS: (NAME)	SEND TAX BILLS TO:	MAP-PARCEL NUMBERS
Paula White	Same as New Owner.	
	(NAME)	
(ADDRESS)	(ADDRESS)	
Nashville, TN 37219		93-6-1-B-502.00 CO
(CITY) (STATE) (ZIP)	(CITY) (STATE) (ZIP)	

Paula's deed for the condo in Nashville
in 2013 a few miles from Jon's family
home in Brentwood. Jon was not yet
divorced.

IN THE CHANCERY COURT FOR THE STATE OF TENNESSEE
21ST JUDICIAL DISTRICT AT FRANKLIN, WILLIAMSON COUNTY

2014 OCT 14 AM 8:43

ENTERED 10-14-14

JONATHAN FRIGA-CAIN,	)	
	)	
Plaintiff,	)	
	)	DOCKET NO: 43116
v.	)	
	)	NOTICE OF ENTRY REQUESTED
ELIZABETH FRIGA-CAIN,	)	
	)	
Defendant.	)	

FINAL DECREE

Jon's final decree of divorce from his wife Liz, Oct. 2014. He met Paula in 2011.

MARRIAGE DISSOLUTION AGREEMENT

THIS AGREEMENT is entered on September 19, 2014 ("MDA Date") by Defendant, ELIZABETH FRIGA-CAIN ("Wife") and Plaintiff, JONATHAN FRIGA –CAIN ("Husband"), subject the following:

1.RECITALS

1. The parties were married on February 17, 1989, in San Rafael, California
2. They separated on February 1, 2014, in Williamson County, Tennessee
3. Differences that the parties are unable to resolve have arisen between them and a Complaint for Divorce filed by Husband in the Chancery Court for the 21st Judicial District in Franklin, Tennessee under the Docket Number 43116 on the grounds of irreconcilable differences.

If they were legally married in Ghana in 2014, the marriage would be legal here in the United States according to the Florida Attorney General's office, so did they stage the "wedding" in 2015? It seems like they did, and then they legally married in 2016 in Apopka, Florida. This is a copy of the official marriage certificate for the year 2016.

You cannot lie on your tax return, so when she filed in 2015 as single, she was for all intents and purposes single, and no legal marriage up to that time seems to have taken place.

"If you can legally file as married, then you must. Married individuals cannot file as single or as the head of a household. Keep in mind the requirements are the same for same-sex marriages. If you were legally married by a state or foreign government, the IRS will expect you to file as married." (Quote from smartasset.com)

Chapter Eight: Strange Collaborators

Mercenary televangelists like Paula White present a distorted and complex picture of Christianity to the unbelieving world.

Franklin Graham, son of the late Billy Graham, would have made a better choice as "spiritual advisor," but he and Pastor Robert Jeffress and Pastor Jack Graham (not related to Billy), all Southern Baptists and Evangelical leaders, set a bad example by compromising with White.

Jack Graham and Robert Jeffress endorsed her book without researching who Paula White really is or what she taught. This is quite a spectacular failure from men who earn their living from the gospel and who have been schooled in the faith. These shepherds have missed the mark and have failed to protect the flock from a wolf. Her acceptance into the mainstream of Evangelical circles comes only because of her position and access to President Trump.

The leaders, Pastors Jack Graham and Robert Jeffress, whom most people trust, refused to speak out about the troubling issues concerning Paula's doctrines. Maybe they compromised to gain access to President Trump through Paula.

Trump needs the Evangelicals' support and votes. Many love him and pray for him, although they might not be aware of some of the serious issues I have stated in this book. Especially when it comes to abortion. On this issue, Evangelicals will desert him for his failures. They also realize his tremendous need for godly counsel, but this woman?

The Bible tells us to pray for our leaders no matter who they are, especially in this day of political upheaval. President Trump wanted Evangelical leaders around him, but going through Paula should not have been the ticket for entry into his circle.

She could have her own agenda for who receives the invitations. If believers really cared about how he is perceived by a hostile media, critics, and millions of Democrats, they would counsel him about the many shortcomings of his "spiritual advisor."

Judging from what I saw on social media, many Christians were appalled when they learned seasoned leaders endorsed her.

The outcry over her appointment by Trump to the position in the White House of Public Liaison was fast and furious. Later, Franklin Graham removed his endorsement of her book, *Something Greater*, from Twitter, and the call went out to Robert Jeffress and Jack Graham to follow suit, but they did not. Jeffress, who is Pastor of First Baptist Dallas, later admitted in an interview with journalist Julie Roys that he had not read the book and was not familiar with Paula White's teachings.

"Jeffress told me in an interview yesterday that White describes her theology as 'Reformed' and '100-percent Trinitarian.' He added that she 'denounces some of the theological error that has been attributed to her.'

"Yet when I asked Jeffress if he's sure that White's theology is orthodox, and that she is not a proponent of the prosperity gospel, Jeffress said, 'All I can say is she claims not to be.'

"I then asked Jeffress whether he's ever investigated what White teaches.

"He answered, 'No, no I'm too busy in my own ministry to launch an investigation.'" By Julie Roys, October 17, 2019

These men endorsed her book hastily once it was published, some without even reading it, and endorsements were already written into the finished manuscript. She was their intermediator to the White House after all.

They are all complicit in promoting her as a legitimate Bible teacher and Christian spokesperson.

Chapter Nine: Same Old Deception

While Paula denies that she manipulates people, many of her fundraising letters tell another story. Here is an example from November 2019 (emphasis in original):

"This email will change your life. I have materials I will rush back to you when I receive your response. *I have a special bottle of anointing oil* that we make from scratch here at PWM, I pray over them personally, believing in faith for breakthrough and deliverance! **I must get you one NOW!** Also, I must get you *a specific teaching series that will go into depth on how to defeat your enemy*, so that you can know the legal maneuvering of the spirit realms. *I am* *making declarations over your victory,* and *I need you to apply the anointing oil to your head, loved ones, house, vehicle, even your checkbook- anywhere you feel attack!!*

"After November, I am agreeing with you that you will enter your season of rest that you may accomplish your dreams.

"But first, you must get what I have to teach you. I feel strongly that a seed of $229 in accordance with 1 Chronicles 22:9 is a breakthrough seed for the month of November.

"It is a turn-around, God-ordained demon slaying abundance-bringing seed. It is a specific seed, numbers are important to God.

($$$$$ emphasis mine)

"Do not take a prophetic instruction lightly! God has been moving us through complete and total breakthrough- and He CAN do it SUDDENLY for you!

"Not only will this seed defeat your enemies, but I also believe it will bring about unexpected blessings.

"If you do not have the means to produce $229, then get a seed of $31 or more. 1 Chronicles 22:9 (22+9=31). But I believe that God was very clear when I received this word that the $229 seed given in faith can break any chains. Like I said, numbers are important to God! ($$$$$ emphasis mine) You have to be able to build towards your future in a season of rest!

"Your life is NEVER going to be the same!

"Love, Your Servant, Paula"

(Paula White-Cain email, November 14, 2019)

It was either the height of arrogance or delusion to put out an appeal letter like that just when you received international attention as a new member of the White House staff. How could you be looking out for the well-being of a man you say you respect and then peddle this kind of garbage out to the public when obviously the interests are your own?

And to add to her arrogance, this remarkably similar appeal letter was sent out in 2014. It was published in a book by Dr. Elisha Coles, Th.D., *Paula White, First Fruits Fleecer*, page 217. I guess her god has Alzheimer's because he did not remember he had already given her this instruction. Even the title is the same: "This email will change your life," but only Jesus can change your life. Change has nothing to do with sending Paula a breakthrough seed.

The only change will be in your bank balance!

While negative press reports about Paula in the secular media are predictable, some of her harshest criticism comes from leaders of the religious right. Columnist Cal Thomas, a former vice-president of the Moral Majority, described Paula's prosperity gospel as heresy in his syndicated column:

"White-Cain is correct on some issues of concern to evangelicals, from Trump's naming of conservative Supreme Court and lower court judges to religious freedom matters, but her seeming worship of President Trump far exceeds biblical norms and her prosperity gospel, which is no gospel at all, fits the definition of heresy: 'Opinion or doctrine at variance with the orthodox or accepted doctrine, especially of a church or religious system.'

"The great danger for the image and what should be the first priority of those who are part of the evangelical community is that they will be seen as worshipping a lesser and even false god than the one they are supposed to be worshipping and serving."

(Cal Thomas, Tuesday, 11/5/2019 *Tribune* content agency, LLC "Who needs spiritual advisors?")

Chapter Ten: History of Ministry and the Downfall

I have included in this book the report that was prepared as part of the Senator Grassley investigation that began in 2007.

It documents the greed and financial mismanagement that led to the end of the White's marriage and the foreclosure, bankruptcy, and bulldozing of almost everything they had built together on sinking sand.

The chapter I wrote in my book *Seed Faith, Can a Man Bribe God? How false teachers manipulate and hypnotize you for offerings* is also included here, and it has been edited for this publication.

In that book, we reveal the tactics the TV evangelists use to solicit money, as well as some of what goes on behind the scenes, and information about their public and private lives

Documented there is the downfall of the White's "ministry" as I witnessed some of it firsthand, reporting on video and visiting the two churches and the four-story administration building that were all later bulldozed.

I followed the story and reported on it for about four years on my internet radio broadcast Prophetic News and YouTube channel, culminating with the chapter in my book.

Now Paula has stepped up her game. She seems to be a self-destructive person, and apparently, she did not learn from her past as she continues her miracle selling, yet she does it with a wider and more critical audience.

Paula said her new husband Jonathan Cain has enough money, and she does not have to work. It would be a blessing if she could enjoy her family and her position and leave God's people alone, but like any junkie, she can't quit. Fame can be a drug. Recognition and adulation can be addicting for a religious leader seeking the spotlight.

Jim Bakker said they should make a movie of her life, and Paula also has been dropping hints, too. You may get what you ask for, and the film could be titled *Paula White, the Female "Elmer Gantry."*

She boasts that history will record her as the first female "clergy" to pray at an Inauguration, but there may be a caveat if the press has its way about how that history will be recorded.

(Edited excerpt from *Seed Faith: Can a Man Bribe God?*)

Paula White arrived on the national scene out of nowhere. I remember that Dwight Thompson's wife, Zonelle, promoted her a long time ago, and she continually became more visible.

While watching CTN one day, there was Paula and her then-husband Randy White on the screen. They would come to our local "Christian" Television Network, CTN, in Clearwater, Florida, with large checks, smiling broadly, and saying they were sowing seeds. Or just maybe they were trying to buy the favor of the station's president for airtime?

They started a church called Tampa Christian Center, which later became

Without Walls. They boasted a congregation of 25,000, although I seriously doubt they ever had that many members because I heard Randy say one Sunday that they counted all the people who came to their feeding programs and giveaways as members, not actual Sunday morning attendees. (Audio was from a sermon by Randy White.)

Paula said her rich relatives on her father's side did not help her widowed mother after her father died, so she went from riches to rags and back to riches.

The story is convoluted. Even her father's suicide story has different versions. She told Larry King in a televised interview in 2007 that the suicide was not pre-meditated, but bad judgment in a moment.

In a sermon that can be heard on YouTube titled *Paula White's False Testimony, Part 1*, she says, "And maybe he didn't directly commit suicide, but he certainly that night left the place. (He was taken by the police from her mother's apartment after a drunken altercation and spent the night in jail. That morning, he had the accident.) And whether it was rage and irresponsibility and drunkenness or whether it was rage and I'm going to do this; the bottom line is he took his life and left a five-year-old girl abandoned."

I do not doubt she suffered greatly from the loss of her father. That is a deep wound, and anyone who has lost a beloved parent feels the void throughout their life.

According to the published newspaper report after the death of Donald Furr, the accident happened in Holly Springs, halfway between Memphis and Tupelo, so it appears he was on his way home to Tupelo.

Paula also claims she bought her trailer with cash from a trust for $37,000, becoming a real estate genius and a multi-millionaire by thirty. I don't know which trailer she is talking about, but the one she bought with Dean had a mortgage, which was later satisfied in March 1990 after Dean sold it in February 1990 for $67,000. (They had already divorced by this time.)

https://youtu.be/2mXsrdKTIfE

FEB 2 2 1990

This Deed

Made this ...12th......... day of ......February................ 19 90, by and between

H. DEAN KNIGHT

party (ies) of the first part, and

his wife, as tenants by the entireties

party (ies) of the second part:

WITNESSETH, that in consideration of the sum of $67,000.00   and other good and valuable considerations, receipt of which is hereby acknowledged, the said party (ies) of the first part do (es) grant and convey unto the party (ies) of the second part in fee simple, all those tracts or parcels of land situate in   Frederick   County, State of Maryland, described as

Lot numbered Three (3) in the subdivision known as "Lots 1, 2, and 3, KNIGHTS DELIGHT" as per plat thereof recorded among the land records of Frederick County, Maryland in Plat Book 8 at plat 38.

1576   433

Paula gave up all her rights to the trailer at the time of her divorce from Dean in 1989 for a $5,000 settlement. She never sold this trailer. Dean did after their divorce.

Release

OF DEED OF TRUST OR MORTGAGE

H. Dean Knight and Paula M. Knight
(Maker of trust or mortgage)

Farmers and Mechanics National Bank   AS RECORDED
(Trustees or mortgagee)

LIBER ___1347___ FOLIO ___0522___

TO ___Charles A. Carlton, P.O. Box 380 Mt. Airy, MD 21771___
File NO. 89-7484

4. REAL PROPERTY: The Wife agrees to convey to the Husband, all of her right, title and interest in the family home located at 4101 Bill Moxley Road, Mt. Airy, Maryland and the Husband does agree to pay unto the Wife the sum of $5000.00 within 120 days of the date of the signing of this Agreement in consideration of the Wife's transferring all of her right, title and interest to the Husband in the above referred to premises.

Then there are the stories about her not having enough food at different times in her adult life; as she opined, she starved for six years.

She once stated she sold the trailer for $90,000 (Which trailer?) and made a good profit, so how did she go hungry at times? There was no record from Bill Moxley Road, Mt. Airy, Maryland, where Paula sold that particular property for $90,000 if you do the property search.

Randy said at one point when they were dating, she was living at home with Admiral Loar and her mother, and Paula was a receptionist at a urologist's office. He also had a government job at the time.

Paula, who seems obsessed with her image, cannot bear criticism. She calls critics haters, yet most of her critics quote her directly, so is she trying to censor herself?

She has tried to have YouTube videos about her removed, but the copyright law offers some protection to the reporters and users.

Since the copyright law has an inclusion built into it called Fair Use, it allows one to use copyrighted material.

As Wikipedia explains:

"For purposes such as criticism, comment, news reporting, teaching (including multiple copies for classroom use), scholarship, or research, which is not an infringement of copyright.

"In determining whether the use made of a work in any particular case is a fair use the factors to be considered shall include: the purpose and character of the use, including whether such use is of a commercial nature or is for nonprofit educational purposes; the nature of the copyrighted work; the amount and substantiality of the portion used in relation to the copyrighted work as a whole; and the effect of the use upon the potential market for or value of the copyrighted work."

YouTube takes your channel down if there are three complaints against it, even before you enter your defense. You are guilty until proven innocent. Maybe Paula learned her lesson when she had to pay Shirley Johnson for malicious prosecution.

Paula has a yearly fundraising event called "First Fruits." Every January, she asks you to give God (Paula) your first month's salary, first week's salary, or one day's salary to appease God, so the rest of the year goes right for you.

Wow, how creative and lucrative. It worked beautifully for a while as the Tampa Tribune reported the Whites took in over $39,000,000 in 2006 and had astronomical debts in other years.

In August 2008, Without Walls defaulted on a $1 million loan due to California-based Evangelical Christian Credit Union, which prompted the credit union to file foreclosure proceedings.

The filing also included a $12 million loan made to the organization in December 2003. (See the Senate report at the end of the book.)

Paula and Randy bought a mansion on Bayshore Boulevard in Tampa and also a condominium at a Trump building on Park Avenue in Manhattan. However, she left New York and returned to her church, Without Walls, in Tampa as it was teetering on bankruptcy. She still owns that condo today.

Also, on the list to benefit was T.D. Jakes, or Daddy to Paula. She refers to Jakes and his wife Serita as her spiritual parents. She previously was invited to preach at Jakes' Mega-Fest meetings, which had been very lucrative for Paula.

So, it seems to seal the deal; she bought Jakes a brand-new Bentley, a car that could cost over $200,000. (According to the Grassley report, in July 2007, the *St. Petersburg Times* reported in an article written by Sherri Day: Paula White indicated she sent Bishop T.D. Jakes a black convertible Bentley for his fiftieth birthday. White did not indicate if the source of the funds used were from her personal income or that of the ministry.)

Some in her congregation may just be getting by financially. Maybe they drive an older car, while Paula and Jon drive in luxury. Their luxurious lifestyle was revealed in their legal battle with Johnson. A public court filing showed the Cain-Frigas purchased a Lamborghini. So, shouldn't her "Daddy" drive a luxury car, too?

White also brings in guest speakers to sell the prosperity gospel to her church. An African prophet told one lady in the congregation to get out her checkbook and write a check for $50,000.

He hit up another couple for $75,000. (See my video on YouTube, "Gangsta Preachers," for the audio.)

And then there are Passover offerings where you must "honor" God by giving money to Paula. However, Jesus is our final Passover offering, and there is no substitution.

You can also sow financial seeds of money to defeat your enemies and get supernatural debt cancellation, where the prosperity preachers tell you God will erase your debts. They even have said the money could suddenly appear in your bank account. The Robin Hood god will take from the rich and give to the poor with the magical seed you sow.

Even your creditors may wipe out your debts with the mighty seed.

That was not the case for Without Walls as the debts continued to rise, and the Lakeland, Florida, building sold at a foreclosure auction, and the other building in Tampa sold just before foreclosure.

Paula said in a CNN interview that she never filed for bankruptcy, but she contributed to the downfall of both churches, as you will see later in the report prepared by the office of Senator Grassley. They owed the Evangelical Christian Credit Union millions.

Paula flew the coop in 2012 to the more profitable digs at the New Destiny Christian Center in Apopka, Florida, still reeling from the drug overdose death of their much-loved Pastor, Zachary Tims.

She left behind the mess in Tampa and Lakeland for her ex-husband Randy to clean up, even though he was hardly in any shape to take on the challenge.

Arrested for drunk driving in 2011, Randy White had a nervous breakdown and eventually wound up on heroin, according to an interview Paula gave on the *Jim Bakker Show* after her book was published. He also went through a string of women during their marriage, which was devastating to the union. (*Something Greater*. Kindle edition, page 124)

You may ask how a pastor can wind up like Randy. We, in the Christian world, know all too well how people can wind up losing their minds like the prodigal son who ate slop with the pigs or King Nebuchadnezzar who ate grass like an ox.

King Nebuchadnezzar was humbled by God for pride, one of the things God hates.

Scripture from the book of Daniel:

Chapter 4: "The same hour was the thing fulfilled upon Nebuchadnezzar: and he was driven from men and did eat grass as oxen, and his body was wet with the dew of heaven, till his hairs were grown like eagles' *feathers* and his nails like birds' *claws*."

According to the testimony of Pastor Chukwuemeka, who was Zachary Tims' real best friend, Paula manipulated her way into New Destiny, even pushing aside Riva Tims, the ex-wife and widow of Zachary, and his four children.

Paula managed to take over and enjoy the spoils of everything the Tims family had built.

Don't let that Botox smile fool ya. Underneath that plastic exterior is someone who calculates her every move.

Pastor Chukmueweka sent the following letter to the congregation at New Destiny in Apopka during the time when Paula was considered for the position of pastor. Paula also threatened to sue him and his board if he did not keep quiet.

"'Now also we beseech you, brethren, get to know those who labor among you [recognize them for what they are...]'" 1 Thessalonians 5:12 (Amplified Bible). I cannot express in words how hurtful and disappointing it is to hear that Paula White may become the new senior pastor of the New Destiny Christian Center in Orlando since the passing of my spiritual son in the Gospel, Dr. Zachary Tims, Jr.

"Upon hearing of this, I sent a text message to Paula White asking her reasons for lying to the church on Sunday, August 21, the day after burying Pastor Zach. My heart aches.

"According to the *Christian Post*, she said, 'As many of you know, Pastor Zach was my spiritual son (lie) and I had known him since I was- I'm 45 years old- and I've known Pastor Zach since I was about 21, 22 years old (lies). We have enjoyed a very fruitful relationship for many, many, many years.'

"The lies are blatant and ridiculously false. Here is the truth- I led Pastor Zach to the Lord in 1991, one year after meeting him in 1990 at Holiday Health and Fitness, where he and I worked. I introduced him to the church and mentored him until 2009.

"I knew him many years before he ever heard of Paula White; four years before he met and married Riva Tims in 1994 (in which I was his best man); all 15 years during their marriage; and through each year transition of the NDCC ministry from the very beginning until he died.

"According to her statement to the church, Paula White would have to have known him since 1989 when he was still in high school and even after he briefly submitted to Randy White as his pastor, he confided to me facts about his relationship with her that would make her the very last choice to replace him as the senior pastor of NDCC if he were alive today.

"The church is being lied to and I am publicizing this so that you can make an informed decision and not allow this atrocity to happen. I admonish you to ask questions about this and demand the truth about her manipulative tactics and why the Board has agreed to submit to her. Call her into accountability because you deserve the truth.

"Regardless of what you have been told, Paula White and the Board have refused to meet with Pastor Riva since Pastor Zach's passing, why? Unethically, she has played dual roles as a counselor, interim pastor, and added insult to injury by despising pastor Riva, and the children without a cause. Dr. Zach's body was not in the ground for 24 hours before she did this. She would have to have known him as her 'spiritual son' at least six years before he got saved in my house. Read his testimony in his books, *Charisma* magazine, TBN past tapings, etc. if you don't believe me. I have no reason to lie on her, but she is lying to you.

"Dr. I.V. Hilliard has withdrawn his support because of her dishonesty.

"I was shunned from having anything to say at Dr. Zach's funeral because the Board omitted my name from the list of pastors who submitted church resolutions – why? I admonish you to stop and think and question these things before you allow her to destroy the ministry that many of you helped to build. For newcomers who do not know of our blended histories as pastors and co-laborers in our ministries, ask those who are still among you who can tell you of our journey.

"If Paula White is named the pastor this coming Sunday, you are forewarned of the sly fox that she truly is- pray and ask questions before she takes control. I know the facts, and I am not afraid to tell you if you want to know more.

"Paula White was never Pastor Zach's spiritual mother. She was never there unless he was either paying her or visiting Without Walls with big checks. I posted this because she did not respond to my text message today in which I told her that without her response I would post this message to the members of NDCC in Orlando. I have yet to receive her response. I am praying for you."

- Dr. R. Douglas Chukwuemeka, Senior Pastor of New Destiny Christian Church,

Laveen, Arizona – Open Letter to the congregation of the New Destiny Christian Center, December 16, 2011

I do not know him personally. I only had a brief telephone conversation with him, but I admire his courage in posting the letter.

The Tampa Tribune published many articles about the rise and fall of Without Walls International Church, including Camillo Gargano's resignation letter. The church accountant described a church in turmoil and reported, "Handling of finances by upper management is contrary with my fiduciary responsibility."

Management did not seem bothered by the financial problems and used "bullying, excessive force, and verbal abuse as a management style," Gargano wrote. "Not only is it unconscionable for me to work in such a hostile environment, but it is also physically and mentally debilitating to work under such stressful circumstances."

(Baird Helgeson and Michelle Bearden, "Financially, Walls are Closing in On Church" *Tampa Tribune*)

Paula made headlines (after her divorce from Randy) with the still-married Benny Hinn as they were photographed in Rome, Italy, by *The National Enquirer*. Benny's divorce had been filed but was not finalized when Benny and Paula jetted off to Rome on separate planes, according to Hinn, for a supposed visit to the Vatican.

They were spotted holding hands. Both later declared in statements on their websites that it was nothing more than a close friendship. It was a major story that put a major crunch on Benny's donations.

Later, when Hinn reunited with his wife, Suzanne, she became a Paula White look-a-like, which was bizarre.

She had the same hairstyle as Paula, and she bleached her black hair blond. Costi Hinn, Benny's nephew, was quoted as saying in a recent statement posted on Twitter that Paula and Benny were at a Hinn family Christmas party before the Rome trip, so apparently, it was more than a friendship. Here is his tweet:

Costi Hinn, October 14, 2019

"But I've shared a family Christmas with her before the divorce was final, then watched them spin the PR lie to millions, twist biblical parameters, and slowly creep back into the mainstream."

Paula also moved to Texas sometime after her divorce to be close to a man named Rick Hawkins, who was a pastor. There were allegations of sexual misconduct by some of the women who attended his church, which generated unwelcome publicity for him. She sold her house in Texas, estimated to be worth over $700,000, and moved to a large home in an exclusive gated community near Orlando. After marrying Jonathan Cain, they bought a house in Apopka.

Paula and Randy purchased the Carpenters Home Church in Lakeland, Florida, in 2007. Once an Assembly of God church built in the 1980s by Karl Strader, the church had a seating capacity of over 9,500, and the property was beautifully situated on over sixty-three acres.

It later became Without Walls Central. There is also a large historic building built in the 1920s with over two hundred rooms, which once was a retirement home for Carpenters. You can see the photos at the end of the book. The Whites planned to use it for a school, among many other plans that fell through.

The Whites had several pastors there. Paula even filed a lawsuit against one pastor, Randy Coggins, when he left, saying he was stealing her sheep. The lawsuit was later dropped.

They later abandoned the properties. The county shut off the power for non-payment of their electric bill for about three years, and the property was finally foreclosed and sold at auction in July 2014. According to Randy White, he had the electricity turned back on briefly, as he was trying to rescue what really could not be salvaged. It was over.

During about a three-year period, the property was continually vandalized. I went there personally in June 2014 to see the damage.

I called Randy in 2011 to tell him about the vandalism, as a friend of mine from Lakeland went there to inspect the property, and she sent me photos. I spoke with his father, Frank White, who was at the Tampa location, and asked if they knew the property was being vandalized. He thanked me and said they would investigate it, but the vandalism continued.

Many of the windows were shattered, and there was flooding from broken pipes. The A/C systems were being scavenged for copper. Graffiti covered some walls, and the drywall in places had been torn down. There was absolute devastation. I will post some links at the end of this book to some YouTube videos of the property damage, before and after, so you can see the documented destruction for yourselves.

Yet the Whites continued to receive salaries, as was documented in the bankruptcy filing. Randy was paid $150,000 one year, yet they would not provide permanent security for property worth over ten million dollars. I also spoke with a real estate agent who was handling the sale, and he said, "The Whites did not have any money for security at the Lakeland site."

According to New York City court records, Paula and Randy had over $900,000 in equity in their Park Avenue condominium, but they were not going to use their own money to save those buildings or pay for security.

They bought it in 2005 from the Trump organization for $3.5 million.

In 2019, they paid off the condominium on Park Avenue for $2,625,000. Both their names were on the satisfaction of mortgage, even though they were divorced.

Detailed Document Information

DOCUMENT ID:	2019121700		CRFN:	2019000.
# of PAGES:	3		REEL-PAGE:	N/A-N/A
DOC. TYPE:	SATISFACTION OF MORTGAGE		FILE NUMBER:	N/A
DOC. DATE:	12/11/2019		RECORDED / FILED:	12/17/2019 3:55:50 PM
DOC. AMOUNT:	$0.00		BOROUGH:	MANHATTAN
% TRANSFERRED:	N/A		RPTT #:	N/A
MESSAGE:	N/A			

PARTY 1

NAME	ADDRESS 1	ADDRESS 2	CITY	
WHITE, RANDY A	` PARK AVENUE `		NEW YORK	
WHITE, PAULA M	⦁ PARK AVENUE		NEW YORK	

They owed many creditors, including $13.9 million to the credit union. The property sold for $2 million at auction, far below what they owed.

The Lakeland Ledger documented the saga in their newspapers. Needless to say, the Whites were not a testimony of Christian integrity. The newspaper accounts are posted online. Anyone can do the searches and read the many written accounts.

Food was left inside the buildings, along with clothing and furniture, and all could have been donated or given away. So much for their ministry to the poor and needy!

The day I was there, someone showed me dozens of photos taken from the inside. I saw abandoned stacks of communion trays, toys, furniture, medical equipment, books, and many more items.

The person showing me the pictures claimed there was clothing piled high to the ceiling in one building. If you search on the internet, there is a video of abandoned buildings and Without Walls. Lakeland is one of the buildings. A baby grand piano sits gathering mold in one frame as they document the destruction of this once-pristine property.

Why talk about the White's financial problems? Because they claim your financial problems can be solved by tithing and sowing money to them for the ministry, yet they were not able to pay their bills.

In 2014, Without Walls settled its debts in bankruptcy court.

She went to work full-time at New Destiny Christian Center, in Apopka, Florida, in 2012, and she severed her ties with the sinking ship in Tampa and Lakeland. The Tampa property was in foreclosure and was purchased a few days before the foreclosure auction.

Randy White met for a while in a high school, and then they moved to an old, moldy building. Yet they still tell the gullible "Give us some money and God will bless you," even though He did not bless them at the time.

Randy pastored a church not too far from the old location, next door to a strip bar, and he still used the same fundraising tactics that led to his previous downfall. As of this writing, Randy resigned as Pastor of Without Walls in 2021 for health reasons.

The former administration building at the Tampa location was about four stories and once housed the Paula White television studios and offices. It was left derelict. Paula said on the *Jim Bakker Show* she spent ten million dollars building her studio. I visited the property twice. I witnessed broken windows, electrical wiring hanging out of the building, and an old dirty mattress sitting by the once-beautiful fountain, a testimony to the judgment of God on the "ministry" of Paula White.

On my second visit, I observed the bulldozers razing the property. Both Tampa buildings were demolished in June 2015. (See YouTube video links at the end of the book.)

The property in Lakeland became a haven for what looked like crackheads and rats, all vandalized through the neglect of Randy and Paula White.

The Lakeland Ledger, Tampa Tribune, and local TV news broadcasts also reported on the collapse of the Whites' ministries.

Without Walls Lakeland, Florida ordered vacated for non-payment of the electric bill. It was ordered unsafe for human occupancy.

(by God Almighty Himself)

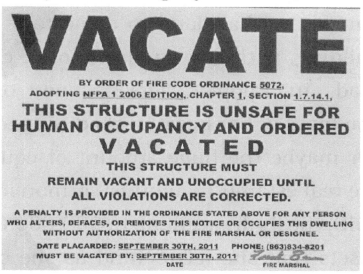

Even though the facts have been documented by many others, Paula did count on the fact that she could serve up her Kool-Aid and stretch the truth to a national television audience, and they would not check the facts for themselves, but those days are over. The national and international media are now watching.

Paula told the crowd at New Destiny that when she came to pastor there, she left behind $60,000,000 in "ASSETS" in Tampa and Lakeland to come to a metal building, with few windows, off a county road, in Apopka, Florida, out of the goodness of her heart in obedience to God. (Or maybe the huge amount of equity in the real estate.) In another sermon in June 2019, the figure went up to $80,000,000 in assets that she left behind as she claims that she put a sacrifice on the altar to come to New Destiny.

Paula failed to mention the massive debts that she left behind.

Now she intends to build her City of Destiny in Apopka. Her son Brad fills in for her on occasion, and she calls him a "phenom." The "phenom" once suggested in a Sunday sermon that maybe Jesus thought about getting married. He always has been paid a substantial sum of money working for Mom, and she even bought him a house next door to hers.

According to the 2011 Senate Finance Committee report, Paula, and Randy's family members (Paula's son and Randy's son, daughter, father, and sister) were paid $420,000, $560,000, $700,000, and $1,075,000 in tax years 2004, 2005, 2006, and 2007, respectively.

She has been bragging for years at every church she has pastored that she will build a city, hospital, and university. In a 2013 sermon, she said the parking lot at City of

Destiny would be paved, and you would no longer get sand in your shoes, but in December 2019, I got sand in my shoes; the parking lot still was not paved. None of her dubious promises are ever fulfilled. As of January 2023, Paula still brags she will build a city, and people will flock to Apopka to be a part of this delusion. Extravagant boasting is used as a motivational trick to get people excited about giving and is nothing but a lot of hot air!

Jon now joins her on the set of her television program, usually playing the piano, and he is a willing participant in his wife's unconventional way of fundraising and deception. He has been on her TV show, *Paula Today*, hawking first fruits offerings and reading testimonials of what remarkable things can happen if you send Paula money. It was so pitiful!

Jon is a multi-millionaire and a member of the rock band Journey. A self-made man, now he seems scripted and robotic as his wife takes the lead and does most of the talking. He is mainly a prop as he plays funeral music in the background while Paula preaches. He is promoted as a "Christian recording artist," but he cannot sing and does so mainly off-key. He once lamented that the band Journey did not let him sing solos, and it has become quite obvious why. Granted, he is a gifted songwriter. Singer, no!

Recently on a Sunday morning, he even had to get his wife's permission to speak. She cut him off because she had to prophesy. Who really wears the pants in that house?

I wonder how Jon will like submitting to Paula as Randy did. These words were immortalized on video as Randy tried to speak at a church service hosted by "Pastor Paula," and she shut him down. He sheepishly said, "I am going to submit to you." I laughed till I cried.

The following articles are from the local Tampa Bay newspapers, and they document some of what happened during the Without Walls years when Paula was married to Randy White.

Quotes from a story by Gary White from the *Lakeland Ledger*, March 16, 2014:

"Without Walls filed for Chapter 11 bankruptcy in federal court in Tampa. The credit union, which says Without Walls owes it $13.9 million on the Lakeland property, began foreclosure proceedings in Bartow's 10th Judicial Circuit in October 2012.

"Without Walls Central, originally known as Carpenter's Home Church, is the largest sanctuary in Polk County with a seating capacity of about 9,500. The church has been dormant since August 2011. Without Walls bankruptcy filing names nearly one hundred creditors."

Michelle Samaad, *Credit Union Times*, June 16, 2014:

"Plagued by a bankruptcy and mounting, unpaid code enforcement fines, a Florida church that received a loan from the Evangelical Christian Credit Union in 2008 is up for auction.

"The auction is scheduled for July 8, 2014. Without Walls, Central is owned by the Tampa-based Without Walls International Church, which filed for

Chapter 11 bankruptcy protection on March 5th owing $29 million to the $1 billion Evangelical Christian Credit Union of Brea, California.

"The Lakeland property was auctioned off in July of 2014 and sold to the credit union that loaned the Whites the money to purchase the property for $2,000,000. The credit union sold it to a development company that demolished the beautiful 9,500-seat church to build senior citizen apartments."

You can go here to see the bankruptcy filing:

UNITED STATES BANKRUPTCY COURT
www.flmb.uscourts.gov

In re: Chapter 11 WITHOUT WALLS INTERNATIONAL CHURCH, INC., Case No. 8:14-bk-2567-MGW

Chapter Eleven: Feeding the Poor

Paula brags about feeding thousands of people millions of pounds of food. Although she does say The City of Destiny is a distribution center when she talks about the program, she uses the phrase "gifts in kind," so who knows what that means? But what is not mentioned on a regular basis is that the church receives grants from Second Harvest and other groups. One year, Second Harvest gave $146,000, in a non-cash grant according to the 990 filed in 2018-2019, and then they donate the food to her.

She also partners with a large group of churches, as many as 150 according to her recent sermons. The City of Destiny is the main distribution center, and the other churches are most likely receiving grants for the donated food too. They also partner with several other companies that supply food and furniture.

Just how much her ministry is spending on food is not known. Feeding people is a wonderful outreach, but in all fairness, to your ministry partners, you should be upfront about where the food is coming from and what you are spending to buy food.

They ask for volunteers to help on the days the food is handed out, so who gets paid for this outreach is another unknown. It can be a lucrative fundraising tool to make you look like you are another Mother Theresa or Evita Peron.

Here is a copy of the 990 from Second Harvest to Operation Love Outreach, which is affiliated with the City of Destiny. The newer 990 for 2020 states they received $113,000 in grants and non-cash assistance. For 2019, it was $146,970.

Paula White

Form 990,Schedule I, Part II, Grants and Other Assistance to Domestic Organizations and Domesti

(a) Name and address of organization or government	(b) EIN	(c) IRC section if applicable	(d) Amount of cash grant	(e) Amount of non-cash assistance
CARING FOR OTHERS 464 PALM ST WINTER GARDEN, FL 34787		501(C)(3)		116,255
OPERATION LOVE OUTREACH THE CITY OF DESTINY 505 EAST MCCORMICK ROAD APOPKA, FL 32703		501(C)(3)		146,970

Conclusion

You may ask, "Could this book affect future elections?" "Could it turn off Evangelicals?" I hope it does, but it is better for Christians to expose this kind of corruption rather than leave the job to the secular media instead of church folk.

Other news outlets could put this information out since it is available to the public on the internet or to anyone who searches for it, and I hope they do.

As for Paula, it's a sad commentary on a life that could have served a greater purpose with the visibility of her public platform. She has been given every opportunity to succeed. In the end, she will have no one to blame but herself, as the controversy of her own making seems to follow her. One day, she will stand before God and give an account for her sins.

Lately, she has been whining about being called a "heretic." Here is the definition from the great 1828 *Webster's Dictionary*:

HER'ETIC, *noun*

1. A person under any religion, but particularly the Christian, who holds and teaches opinions repugnant to the established faith, or that which is made the standard of orthodoxy. In strictness, among Christians, a person who holds and avows religious opinions contrary to the doctrines of Scripture, the only rule of faith and practice.

2. Any one who maintains erroneous opinions.

TITUS 3:10

"A man that is an heretick after the first and second admonition reject;"

Guillermo Maldonado, a "pastor" from Miami, held a conference recently, and Paula was one of the "entertainers" he used to do the fundraising. She had the vast crowd dance a wild freedom dance, then put them back into bondage by saying they were to sow $1000 to get miracles.

That is one of the reasons Paula White is a heretic. The Lord Jesus Christ does not talk like that, and it is contrary to the doctrines of scripture.

Here is how Jesus talks:
Matthew 7:6-12

"⁶Give not that which is holy unto the dogs, neither cast ye your pearls before swine, lest they trample them under their feet and turn again and rend you. Ask, and it shall be given you; seek, and ye shall find; knock, and it shall be opened unto you: For everyone that asketh receiveth; and he that seeketh findeth; and to him that knocketh it shall be opened.

"Or what man is there of you, whom if his son ask bread, will he give him a stone? Or if he ask a fish, will he give him a serpent? If ye then, being evil, know how to give good gifts unto your children, how much more shall your Father which is in heaven give good things to them that ask him? Therefore all things whatsoever ye that men should do to you, do ye even so to them: for this is the law and the prophets."

Paula moans because she says people who have never had a conversation with her have pre-judged her and called her a heretic, yet she is snared by the words of her mouth.

What about the Mafia Don god whom she says removes his protection if you do not pay him ten percent? There is no proof anywhere in Scripture that tithing was ever money. Jesus never tithed money or ever asked for financial tithes during his earthly ministry. Since He was the Living Word, I guess He would know, and the Lord Jesus never asked for money on feast days.

There will be false brethren among us, and we live in a time of so much turmoil. We have all been through so many trials these last few years. The rich and famous preachers will turn on the remnant church, so as good Bereans, we should be able to recognize false doctrine when we hear it. People who pose as Christians are a huge threat to biblical truth and are wolves in sheep's clothing. Just like the

Reformers of old, we reject heresy and have no fellowship with the unfruitful works of darkness.

People who sell miracles bring a reproach to the cause of Christ. They make Christians look foolish and greedy. While so many have been tremendously gifted to preach, sing, and hold the attention of a crowd, they have misused their gifts to satisfy their lust and greed. They cannot be separated from the world.

When false brethren portray God Almighty and Jesus Christ as two heavenly beings who are sitting on their thrones waiting to see money pass from your hand to theirs, that is ludicrous.

At this time, Paula White has no place in real Christian ministry. Spiritual advisor to the President of the United States? Chair of American Values? God help us! Life can be stranger than fiction, and this story truly is!!

The Grassley Report

Senate Finance Committee, Minority Staff Review of Without Walls International Church Paula White Ministries (Prepared by Lynda F. Simmons) Paula and Randy White

Introduction

The Committee's initial letter was addressed to Without Walls International Church (WWIC) and Paula White Ministries (PWM). WWIC was formed in Tampa, FL, by Randy and Paula White. Paula White Ministries (PWM), the media division of the organization, was formed in 2001. WWIC is supported primarily through contributions from its congregants and PWM is supported through partnership offerings from worldwide viewers and the sales of ministry-related materials through television, direct mail, website, and speaking engagements.1

Paula White is a partner and the president of Paula White Ministries. 2

In August 2007 prior to the initiation of the Senate Finance Committee investigation, Randy and Paula White announced their plans to divorce. After Paula's departure, Randy White was the sole senior pastor at WWIC, and Paula continued to operate PWM. In August 2008, the WWIC defaulted on a $1 million bank loan but was able to come out of foreclosure in March 2009.

In July 2009, Randy White stepped down as senior pastor of WWIC and Paula returned to the organization. To date, Paula is the senior pastor of WWIC.

WWIC provided responses to some of the Committee questions. Committee staff discussed securing the additional responses with WWIC's attorneys. Randy White participated in one of these conversations. Randy and the attorneys expressed an interest in complying fully but explained that they continued to have concerns about confidentiality and violation of constitutional protections. Staff provided the same assurances that were provided to the other churches but were still unable to secure the requested information. As a result, Committee staff ceased communicating with WWIC and its attorneys and began obtaining information from public records and third parties, including insiders.

Employee Confidentiality Agreements

As a term of employment, WWIC requires that employees sign a confidentiality agreement which prevents them from ever discussing anything pertaining to the organization.

Several former WWIC staff members wanted to speak with committee staff but were afraid of being sued by the church. Staff is aware of at least one former employee who received a letter from WWIC's attorneys reminding them of the confidentiality agreement.

Governance

Officers, Directors, Trustees, and Key Employees

1 Church submission dated March 28, 2008.

2 Trinity Foundation, Inc.

Page 2 of 13

The WWIC provided with its board of directors for the years 2004, 2005, and 2006. According to the response Randy was the Chairman and President for those years and Paula was the Vice-President and Secretary. The other individuals listed did not appear to be related to the Whites.

Board Meetings

According to the information provided by WWIC, WWIC did conduct board meetings, which all board members generally attended. All board meetings were conducted via teleconference and there were no costs associated with these annual meetings.

A former staff member familiar with the board of directors stated that all decisions concerning WWIC and particularly WWIC finances were made by the Whites and Norva Carrington, the Chief Financial Officer. Board members typically found out after the fact.3

In addition, according to the 2006 financial statement provided by WWIC, one board member was paid $15,000 for his services as a guest speaker in 2005.

Per former board member Alrick Clark, he has been friends with Randy and Paula White since the Whites began their ministry in Tampa. Clark lives in another state and was not an active participant in many board decisions and has limited knowledge concerning many financial decisions. Clark provided the following statements:

The Whites purchased their home in Tampa Bay and probably received a housing allowance from the church.

The church purchased a jet that was not a sound investment. Therefore, it ended up leasing a jet instead. When the jet was not being used, the church leased the jet to others.

He was not informed of the decision to put the church up for sale.

He resigned from the board in January 2008, citing not being informed on important matters.

In a DVD provided by a third-party informant, Paula White states to an audience that deacons and boards should not run pastors.

Organizational Structure

Without Walls International Church (WWIC) and Paula White Ministries consolidated audited financial reports were prepared by Lewis, Birch & Ricardo, LLC of Clearwater, Florida. The external audit was completed in April of 2007.

These statements were submitted to the Committee and, at one time, were posted on their websites. However, they are no longer publicly available.

The following is from the Auditor's Notes to the financial statements obtained from the website. 3 Third Party Informant Without Walls International Church, Inc.

Page 3 of 13

"The combined financial statements of Without Walls International Church, Inc. and Affiliates include the accounts of Without Walls International Church, Inc. (WWIC); Spirit Led, LLC (Spirit Led), a limited liability company organized in the State of Delaware, and KABB Enterprises, LLC (KABB), a limited liability company organized in the state of Florida.

WWIC is the sole member of both Spirit Led and KABB. Since these entities are under common control, they are collectively referred to as Without Walls International Church, Inc., and Affiliates.

Accordingly, and all of the intercompany transactions have been eliminated in the consolidation.

Spirit Led, LLC and KABB Enterprises, LLC are subsidiaries of WWIC." Related Party Transactions

It is a common practice for a church to purchase the books, tapes, CDs, and DVDs of a minister to sell to third parties. However, it was reported to the committee by an insider that Randy and Paula White insisted that the organization purchase a certain amount of their products to sell.4

According to the Auditor's Notes to the audited financial statements previously mentioned, during 2005 and 2006 WWIC made inventory purchases of $541,000 and $330,000, respectively, from two companies owned by Randy and Paula White. In those same years, WWIC also made rental payments of $24,000 and $3,000, respectively, to Randy and Paula

White. No further details regarding these transactions are provided.

Related Entities

According to the response provided by WWIC, WWIC is a consolidated entity comprised of two local congregations, a media ministry, and two limited liability corporations (LLC) and there are no affiliated churches or integrated auxiliaries.

The two congregations are Without Walls International Church, Inc. and Without Walls Central. The media ministry is Paula White Ministries, and the two LLCs are Spirit Led and KABB Enterprises.

Per the audited financial statements, WWIC is the sole member of Spirit Led, LLC and KABB Enterprises, LLC. "As such, the Church accounted for its investments in Spirit Led and KABB under the principles of accounting applicable to investments in subsidiaries." The WWIC/PWM did not provide any other information regarding Spirit-Led or KABB Enterprises.

Per the Florida Department of State website, KABB Enterprises, Inc. and KABB Enterprises, LLC are two entities registered using the address of WWIC. WWIC is the managing member of the LLC and Randy, and Paula White are corporate officers of KABB Enterprises, Inc. KABB Enterprises Inc. is registered as a for-profit. The articles of incorporation do not indicate the purpose of the corporation. Third-Party Informant C

Page 4 of 13

According to a former employee, KABB was set up by the Whites for WWIC to purchase a Days Inn motel.5

The Church made a down payment that was eventually lost since the sale never went through.6

KABB was administratively dissolved by the state on 10/01/2004 for failure to file an administrative report.7

Spirit Led, LLC is not registered in the state of Florida and there is little information available about this entity. Per the Director of Operations for Venice Jet Center, formerly known as, Triple Diamond, Venice currently sells jet fuel to Spirit Led, LLC.

Other nonprofits related to WWIC (not provided by WWIC) According to the Florida Department of State records, the following nonprofits that list Randy and/or Paula as directors, are operating using the address for WWIC.

Youth With a Vision, Inc.

PWM Life Center, Inc.

Institute for Community Development, Inc.

Paula White Enterprises, Inc.

Destiny Ministries, Inc.

In addition, Norva Covington, WWIC's CFO, is listed as an officer for all but Youth With a Vision, Inc.

For-profits using the WWIC address (not provided by WWIC) According to the Florida Department of State records, the following for-profit companies that list Randy and/or Paula as officers are operating using the address for WWIC

E&R Music, LLC

Raw Reality Enterprises, Inc.

Ramp Corporation

Identity Records, LLC - according to a former employee, Identity Records was created to record and sell CDs featuring the WWIC choir members.

The assets of the organization were used to make the CD and the sales proceeds went to Identity Records, LLC.

In addition, Norva Covington is also listed as an officer for all but Ramp Corporation.

5   Third Party Informant B

6   Ibid

7   November 2008 research, www.sunbiz.org

Page 5 of 13

Other Nonprofits associated with Randy White (not provided by the organization) According to the Florida Department of

State records, One Less, Inc. and South Tampa Christian Center Foundation, Inc. are corporations associated with Randy White. Randy is noted as a director and registered agent, respectively.

WWIC Affiliates

Per the response to the Committee, there are no WWIC affiliates. However, according to WWIC's website in 2008, an organization or a person can join the Without Walls Ministerial Alliance and become an affiliate. The website provided a list of benefits and an application to become an affiliate. According to the website, in 2008 there were over two hundred affiliates worldwide. As of January 2011, anyone interested in becoming a WWIC affiliate is directed to call the church for information.

Integrated Auxiliaries

Per the information provided by WWIC, there are no integrated auxiliaries.

Finances Audited

Financial Statements

Select Items from WWIC

Audited Financial

Statements:

Page 6 of 13

Support and Revenue
(Author's Note)

How do you take in over $75,000,000 in revenue and wind up bankrupt? And that was revenue for just three years.

Table 1 Tithes and Offerings

$16,382,365.00	2004
$ 23,101,001.00	2005
$35,269,657.00	2006

Product Sales*

$ 3,126,275.00	2004
$2,991,433.00	2005
$2,795,943.00	2006

Conferences and events

$1,519,144.00	2004
$1,696,259.00	2005
$1,208,597.00	2006

Total Support and Revenue

$ 21,620,750.00	2004
$ 28,362,192.00	2005
$ 39,933,163.00	2006

Total Expenses
Specific Expenses of Note
Housing Allowances

$713,779.00	2005
$883,120.00	2006

Advertising and Print Media

$1,230,746.00	2005
$2,031,861.00	2006

Airtime

$6,536,246.00	2005
$8,757,318.00	2006

Travel and Transportation

$2,417,212.00	2005 - 2006

Interest and Financing Costs

$1,638,123.00	2005
$1,283,658.00	2006

Other Item
Long-Term Debt

$ 13,273,490.00	2004
$ 22,507,150.00	2005

Airplane Lease

$ 2,659,079.00	2004
$ 1,221,784.00	2005

*Net cost of goods sold

In response to question 4 from the Committee under "Other" WWIC indicated that Randy White, Paula White, and Norva Carrington determine how the funds of WWIC and PWM are spent. The response went on to say that in regard to both operational and financial, these expenditures are subject to the oversight of the Board of Directors. This is once again in conflict with statements given by Alick Clarke.

In an interview with the Tampa Tribune, former organization accountant Camillo Gargano stated he resigned his position because "handling of finances by upper management is contrary with my fiduciary responsibility." He also stated that management did not seem bothered by the financial problems, and used "bullying, excessive force, and verbal abuse as a management style."

Gargano resigned after Randy White ordered him to pay White's $24,000 personal American Express bill, even though it would mean the ministry couldn't make payroll for the week. A part of the expenses charged on the American Express bill was a $13,000 payment for mirrors installed in WWIC. The rest included personal expenses that White told Gargano he would pay back to the ministry.8

Compensation

8 Baird Helgeson and Michelle Bearden, "Financially, Walls are Closing in On Church" Tampa Tribune Without Walls International Church.

Salary

The organization did not answer any of the questions related to Executive Compensation. However, according to former board member Alick Clark, around 2004 and 2005 Clark received a compensation package prepared by a third party that indicated the Whites were entitled to approximately $5 million in total compensation. Clark could not specifically recall the company that prepared the package.

There are no published reports of the total compensation received by the Whites and this information is not separately listed in the audited financial statements provided to the Committee. An insider familiar with WWIC finances stated that

Randy and Paula White each received compensation in excess of $1,000,000. 9

Compensation Committee

According to the response given by the organization, WWIC, and Paula White Ministries does not have a compensation committee. Although the organization did not provide the name and address of persons or entities that provided compensation studies, in the board minutes provided by the organization

Dated 11/19/2004, it states that the Chairman of the Board (Randy White) presented a compensation study completed by The Strategic Compensation Group of America.

The compensation study included "amounts of compensation, bonuses, cost of living adjustments, other forms of compensation, benefits and similar features involving the pay scale and overall compensation structure of the church." The compensation package that was presented was subsequently approved.

In response to question #4 under "Other", WWIC stated that "all members of the Board of Directors exercise voting rights." It is not clear, but it appears that Randy and Paula White did not recuse themselves when voting on their own compensation.

Honorariums

The following is from the Auditor's Notes to the financial statements.

"The senior pastors, representing themselves and not the Church, at times preach and speak at other churches and venues.

For those engagements where the pastors are representing themselves, the pastors typically receive honorariums from the host church. These honorariums are passed through the Church as a revenue item and then as an expense.

The travel expense associated with these activities that may initially be incurred by the Church is fully reimbursed by the host church. The senior pastors also receive gifts and love offerings that are passed through the church."

9 Ibid

Page 8 of 13

The auditor's notes do not say how or if these honorariums, gifts, and love offerings are reported to the IRS. Honorariums are payments in cash or checks for the service conducted by a minister.

Parsonage/Housing Allowance

According to Hillsborough County property records, from 2002 until their divorce in August of 2007, the Whites owned 4301 Bayshore Boulevard, Tampa, FL, an 8,072 sq. ft. home located in the very prestigious area of Bayshore. The residence has a waterfront view of Tampa Bay. According to Hillsborough County records, the 2008 market value of the home is $2,681,211. The Whites purchased the property in 2002 and borrowed 2 million dollars from SunTrust Bank. An insider told Committee staff that an accounting firm hired by WWIC told the Whites to purchase the largest house they could find. In the spring of 2003, the Whites hired a pool contractor to put a new inground concrete pool and spa at this residence.10

A recent aerial view of the residence indicates the pool was completed. As of December 2008, the registered owner of the Bayshore Boulevard home is Randy White.11

According to an insider, Randy and Paula White also purchased a $3.5 million condo at Trump Park Avenue in New York City.12

The total cost of the condo was $3.5 million, however, only $2,625,000 was financed so it appears the down payment was $925,000.13

WWIC did not provide any information related to possible housing allowances being paid for the residence on Bayshore Drive and the Trump Park Avenue condo.

However, an insider familiar with WWIC finances stated that housing allowances for both residences were paid from WWIC/PWM funds.14

According to the audited financial statements for tax years 2005 and 2006, WWIC paid total housing allowances of $713,779 and $883,120, respectively.

Hillsborough County, Clerk of the Court Hillsborough County Property Appraiser 10

10 Third Party Informant C

11 NYC Department of Finance, Office of The City Register

12 Third Party Informant B

Page 9 of 13

The organization did not provide any information regarding the vehicle allowances being paid for Randy and Paula White. An insider familiar with WWIC finances indicated that in the past WWIC would.

Vehicles driven by Randy White as of July 2008. One vehicle is a late-model Mercedes Benz, and the other is a 2007 Bentley convertible.

5 Third Party Informant B

In addition, a former insider stated that WWIC at one time purchased a car for Norva Carrington. The car was in the name of WWIC but was used exclusively by Norva Carrington.16

Other Benefits

An insider familiar with WWIC finances stated that the Whites used WWIC credit cards and checking accounts to pay for many of their personal expenses such as gas, meals, clothing, and other personal items.17

Randy would promise to pay WWIC back but did not reimburse the organization for these personal expenses.18

Randy incurred expenses on his personal credit card totaling approximately $24,000, of which $13,000 was the cost of mirrors for WWIC. The remaining balance was for personal expenses. Randy insisted that WWIC pay the entire credit card bill even though there were insufficient funds in the WWIC bank account to cover payroll.19

Two persons traveled with Randy White, Joey, and Christopher Capnoplous. 20

They were responsible for paying any travel expenses incurred by Randy White.21

They would then request reimbursement from WWIC. As long as there were receipts, WWIC would pay for the expenses.22

A ministry insider indicated that the Whites chartered jets for personal use and the ministry paid for these Ibid

16   Ibid

17   Ibid

18   Baird Helgeson and Michelle Bearden, "Financially, Walls are Closing in On Church" Tampa Tribune

19   Third Party Informant C

20   Ibid

21   Ibid

Page 11 of 13

For example, the Whites chartered a jet for a trip to Las Vegas to attend a boxing match which was paid for by WWIC.24

Compensation to Relatives

In response to question #2 under "Other" in the Committee letter dated November 5, 2007, the organization gave partial answers. It provided the name and relationship of each related party but did not give the specific amounts received by each.

Information provided by WWIC indicates that WWIC the organization paid family members of Randy and Paula White, including Paula's son and Randy's son, daughter, father, and sister, up to $420,000, $560,000, $700,000, and $1,075,000 in tax years 2004, 2005, 2006 and 2007, respectively.

Real and Personal Property

Real Estate

Per the response to the Committee, there are no overseas bank accounts or investments belonging to WWIC, PWM, or any of its integrated auxiliaries and related entities for the years 2004 to the present.

Per the response to the Committee, WWIC owns five properties, four in Florida and one in California. The four in Florida were purchased by WWIC and the one in California was donated to WWIC in 2005.

Aircraft

Per the response to the Committee, "the ministry" owns a 1969 Gulfstream GII, Model Number N374PS. It is not clear whether the term ministry here refers to WWIC or PWM. The response further states that the aircraft was purchased in January 2006 for $1,200,000.00. During the calendar year 2004, the ministry used chartered flights and "dry leased" aircraft. In 2004 and 2005, any aircraft that were leased were rented from various private leasing companies.

For the years 2004 and 2005, chartered flights were booked through two other private companies. Per the organization, the leasing and charter companies did not provide WWIC with the flight records. The organization failed to provide the cost of leasing aircraft that was used by the ministry. Per a third-party informant, a private company sells fuel to WWIC's

Spirit Led, LLC. 25

An insider stated that the Whites chartered jets for personal use and charged the ministry. The insider recalled one charter to Las Vegas where the Whites took several sports personalities for a boxing match.

The tickets for the boxing match in Las Vegas were for several sports personalities including Gary Sheffield, Darryl Strawberry, Michael Pittman, Anthony Telford, and Juan Long.

23 Third Party Informant B

24 Ibid

25 Third-Party Informant D

The cost of the tickets for the boxing match alone was between $17,000 and $18,000. The Whites used the WWIC American Express to pay for the trip, including the hotel costs.26

A former business associate stated that the Whites used charter jet flights, primarily a Lear 35A that was registered as N405GJ.27 The former associate indicated that the jet was primarily used by Paula and was flown extensively, sometimes as much as 20 hours a week. 28 In addition, the jet was often flown to the islands.29 According to the former business associate, the Whites would depart on a flight plan that was filed to the islands.30

Occasionally, when they left US airspace, they would cancel their original flight plan and re-file a second flight plan to the Cayman Islands while in the air.31

They would do the same procedure on their return.32

The Whites would also use the aircraft of other televangelists such as Jesse Duplantis and Benny Hinn.33

Intellectual Property Rights

In response to question 3 under "Other", the organization indicated that the question goes "beyond the scope of the Senate Finance Committee's investigation into tax-exempt organizations.

Gifts

There is no published information concerning any gifts to the Whites. However, a ministry insider told Committee staff that during an organization service, the Whites asked members to bring their jewelry to the altar to give as an offering.

At a later date, at least one item given as an offering was placed in the Whites' personal safe. 34

Employment Agreements

WWIC provided the Committee with employment agreements for Randy and Paula White. The following are highlights of the agreements: Randy White is the founder of the church and serves as the President, Chief Executive Officer, Senior Pastor, Spiritual Overseer, and Bishop.

- Paula is Co-Founder and serves as Vice-President, Secretary, and Senior Pastor/Co-Pastor.

Employment continues until termination by the Board but there is no indication of who can initiate termination. - compensation shall be determined in accordance with IRS rules. 26 Third Party Informant B 27 Trinity Foundation Inc.

28   **Ibid**

29   **Ibid**

30   **Ibid**

31   **Ibid**

32   **Ibid**

33   **Ibid**

34   **Third Party Informant B**

35

- compensation can be deferred, and discretionary bonuses are authorized

- intellectual property rights are owned by the employees but there is a requirement to disclose to the Board of Directors, all ideas, concepts, programs, methods, plans, developments, or improvements, developed by employees, that relate directly or indirectly to WWIC's business.

They choose their vehicle and whether it will be leased or purchased

Use of Ministry Assets

In August of 2008, the organization defaulted on a $1 million loan due to California-based Evangelical Christian Credit Union which prompted the credit union to file foreclosure proceedings. The filing also included a $12 million loan made to the organization in December of 2003.35

In an article written by Sherri Day of the St. Petersburg Times in July of 2007, Paula White indicated she sent Bishop T.D. Jakes a black convertible Bentley for his 50th birthday. White did not indicate if the source of the funds used were from her personal income or that of the ministry.36

An insider stated that Randy White would fly to California twice a month for unknown reasons. The organization owns a piece of property in California that was donated; however, the organization had no active plans for the property.

White flew a commercial jet, but WWIC covered all his expenses.37

In addition, Randy White placed his girlfriend and her parents on payroll and gave them retroactive pay. Randy White also authorized organization Pastor Jimmy Higgins to take a leave of absence. It was later determined that Higgins had plastic surgery that was paid for by WWIC.38

Eddie L. Long of New Birth Missionary Baptist Church of Atlanta conducted a service at WWIC in 2008. Long charged WWIC $7,500.00 for jet fuel for his private aircraft. In addition, WWIC covered the costs of hotel expenses and paid Long $15,000 for being a guest minister.39

35 Baird Helgeson and Michelle Bearden, "Financially, Walls Are Closing In On Church" Tampa Tribune

36 Sherri Day, "Questions Tarnish Rise To Top"
St. Petersburg Times

37 Third-Party Informant E

38 Ibid

Photos

Zachary Tims

The former pastor of New Destiny before his death. Now the City of Destiny with Paula as pastor.

The White House

The City of Destiny now

Without Walls Church, Tampa boarded
up before the demolition

Vandalism at Without Walls Lakeland

Deserted administration building Tampa

The auction - Lakeland Church

Randy's church after the fall

Vandalized buildings Lakeland

Vandalized Lakeland

Broken windows and dilapidated
buildings, Lakeland

Deserted Tampa

Deserted administration building, Tampa

Randy White's new building, Tampa
He no longer pastors this church

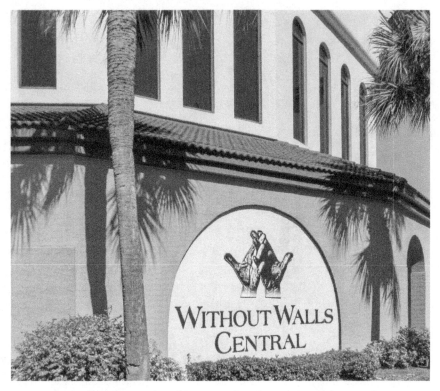

Without Walls Lakeland, Florida

Without Walls Lakeland, Florida, before demolition

VIEW FROM THE DRIVE

The old Carpenters Union home in
Lakeland, Florida it was part of the
White's property

Deserted television studio and
administration building Tampa

Paula's trailer on Bill Moxley Road

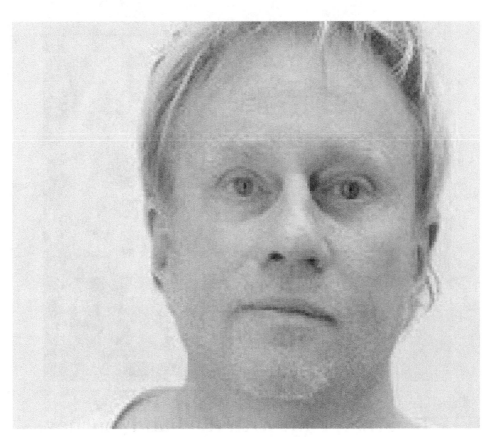

Randy White mugshot from drunk
driving arrest in 2011

Jonathan Cain with the band Journey,
third husband of Paula
White, second from the left
(The band has no affiliation with Paula
White Ministries, as far as I know, other
than Paula is married to a band member.)

Photo by Matt Becker –
(Transferred from en. Wikipedia, CC BY
3.0,
https://commons.wikimedia.org/w/index.
php?curid=6365617)

Matt has no affiliation with this book or
the author.
The majority of the photos in this book
were taken by the author.
And some are official White House
photos in the public domain.

Paula White on the National Day of Prayer

Paula White and Jonathan Cain at
the White House

Paula White at White House dinner

Melania Trump, Jerry Falwell Jr. at
Evangelical Leaders' dinner

Jonathan Cain with Melania Trump
at White House dinner

Donald Trump walks out to take his
oath of office

President Trump and Melania visit
the Pope John Paul memorial in
Washington, D.C.

Trump kneels before a relic of Pope
John Paul's blood

Video Links

Paula and Jon talking about watching porn:

https://youtu.be/UMbXrL7q1zU

Paula "You love that booty" -
Talks about having sex at 8 years old:
https://youtu.be/OW2gc3Kgg_4

Paula talks about her father's death or "maybe he didn't directly commit suicide."
Talks about all the businesses her family owned:
https://youtu.be/zfWsM2EcRjA

Paula talks about selling her trailer and becoming a real estate genius
https://youtu.be/JNbFkULhBnw

Paula says she starves for the next six years of her life - after the age of 18. She also starts her real estate business at 18. Becomes a millionaire at age 30:
https://youtu.be/2mXsrdKTIfE

The demolition of the Lakeland Church:
https://youtu.be/2u8ZBynNMCA

The vandalism and ruins of the abandoned Lakeland church:
https://youtu.be/znvcpk560y8

Demolition of the Tampa Church:
https://youtu.be/cdWaTIbBx_I

Paula visits God's throne room:
https://youtu.be/negvrZq5tBE

Paula White satanic pregnancies:

https://youtu.be/TR_slS9qxQs

Paula White called Divine Mother:

https://youtu.be/jf221RbcrDo

propheticnews.com, my website:

http://www.propheticnews.com

Prophetic News Radio
On Spreaker

https://www.spreaker.com/show/propheti
c-news-radio

https://youtu.be/YMC7jrhJTdE
Did Paula White and Jonathan Cain
commit
Adultery?

Links to Articles About Paula White

Paula White and Ethics, Richard W. Painter

Newsweek - By Jason Lemon on 11/13/19 at 10:55 AM EST

https://www.newsweek.com/bush-ethics-lawyer-paulawhite-1471524

Pastor claims he caught Trump spiritual adviser Paula White stealing from her own church's collection plate:

https://www.rawstory.com/2017/05/pastor-claims-he-caught-trump-spiritual-adviser-paula-white-stealing-from-her-own-church-collection-plate/

Paula and Randy White: Of Faith, Fame & Fortune

Tampa Tribune/May 20, 2007

By Michelle Bearden and Baird Helgeson

Paula and Randy White: Of Faith, Fame & Fortune (culteducation.com)

Paula White urges her followers to pay her instead of their bills:

https://www.newsweek.com/trumps-spiritual-adviser-paula-white-warns-christians-give-church-before-paying-their-1487867

She led Trump to Christ: The rise of the televangelist who advises the White House – *The Washington Post*

https://www.amazon.com/Tithing-Scriptural-Command-Church-ebook/dp/B00HB77ZFI

Russell Kelly Ph.D.: *Should the Church Teach Tithing?*

https://www.amazon.com/Should-Tithing-Theologians-Conclusions-Doctrine/dp/0595159788

Article by Russell Kelly Ph.D. on first fruits: "First fruits were never tithes":

http://www.tithing-russkelly.com/id240.html

Other Books by Susan Puzio

Paula White Financial Information
(Public Documents)

That wasn't enough, $646,000. From 2014 for Pastor's salary.

There was more on Pastor Appreciation Day, and there are also birthday offerings.

234

Form **8275** (Rev. August 2013) Department of the Treasury Internal Revenue Service	**Disclosure Statement** Do not use this form to disclose items or positions that are contrary to Treasury regulations. Instead, use Form 8275-R, Regulation Disclosure Statement. ▶ Information about Form 8275 and its separate instructions is at *www.irs.gov/form8275.* ▶ Attach to your tax return.	OMB No. 1545-0889 Attachment Sequence No. 92

Name(s) shown on return

PAULA M. WHITE

Identifying number shown on return

▉▉▉-6232

If Form 8275 relates to an information return for a foreign entity (for example, Form 5471), enter:

Name of foreign entity ▶

Employer identification number, if any ▶

Reference ID number (see instructions) ▶

Part I   General Information (see instructions)

(a) Rev. Rul., Rev. Proc., etc.	(b) Item or Group of Items	(c) Detailed Description of Items	(d) Form or Schedule	(e) Line No.	(f) Amount
1	N/A	PASTOR APPRECIATION GIFTS	1040	7	65,658.
2					

Pastor Appreciation offering $65,658.00

They take one every year.

Special thanks to Shirley Johnson, who brilliantly acted as her own attorney with no formal training and won her case against all of Paula's high-powered attorneys. Thus, we have these documents. Thanks to the *Washington Post* and the Trinity Foundation for filing the

motions to get these financial documents unsealed from the Orlando court.

Form 1116	U.S. and Foreign Source Income Summary			
NAME				
PAULA M. WHITE				▓▓-6232
INCOME TYPE		TOTAL	U.S.	FOREIGN PASSIVE
Compensation		646,211.	646,211.	
Dividends/Distributions	SEE STATEMENT 32	19,479.	9,263.	10,216.
Interest		843.	843.	
Capital Gains		42,663.	42,663.	
Business/Profession				
Rent/Royalty		9,788.	9,788.	
State/Local Refunds				
Partnership/S Corporation		107,576.	107,576.	
Trust/Estate				
Other Income				
Gross Income		826,560.	816,344.	10,216.
Less:				
Section 911 Exclusion				
Capital Losses		45,663.	45,663.	
Capital Gains Tax Adjustment				4,769.
Total Income - Form 1116		780,897.	770,681.	5,447.

.

Paula Michelle White

Statement of Financial Condition

December 31, 2017

Assets	
Cash and Investments	1,794,000
Personal Effects	30,000
Vehicles	159,000
Real Estate and Personal Residences	4,554,000
Investments in Closely Held Businesses	1,350,000
Total Assets	7,887,000

New Destiny Assets December 31, 2017

Contributions, Support, and Revenue	
Tithes and Offerings	4,820,764
Other	524,730
Net Assets Less Expenses End of Year	10,256,624

Paula cannot be removed as Pastor; she put herself in for life. If anything happens to Paula, her son, Bradley, will become the pastor. (from her by-laws).

Section 5. Resignation, Removal, Succession, of Pastor-President

(a) *Resignation.*

If the Pastor-President voluntarily resigns she may designate her successor.

(b) *Removal.*

The Pastor-President shall serve as President and a member of the Board of Directors of the church until her death or resignation, and without the need of election or appointment. She shall not be subject to <u>*removal.*</u>

(c) *Death.*

Upon the death of the Pastor-President, she shall be succeeded in the office of Pastor-President and as a director by her son, <u>*Brad Knight.*</u>

Two-Year Comparison Worksheet

2014

Name(s) as shown on return			Social security number
PAULA M. WHITE			-6232

2013 Filing Status SINGLE   2014 Filing Status SINGLE

2013 Tax Bracket 0.0%   2014 Tax Bracket 39.6%

Description	Tax Year 2013	Tax Year 2014	Increase (Decrease)
WAGES, SALARIES, AND TIPS	513,410.	646,211.	132,801.
SCHEDULE B - TAXABLE INTEREST	949.	843.	-106.
SCHEDULE B - ORDINARY DIVIDENDS	13,422.	19,479.	6,057.
SCHEDULE B - QUALIFIED DIVIDENDS	13,079.	18,721.	5,642.
SCHEDULE D (CAPITAL GAIN/LOSS)	-3,000.	-3,000.	
FORM 4797 (OTHER GAINS OR LOSSES)	-453,261.	0.	453,261.
SCHEDULE E (RENTAL AND PASSTHROUGH)	-113,975.	107,630.	221,605.
OTHER INCOME	400.	-69,720.	-70,120.
TOTAL INCOME	-42,055.	701,443.	743,498.
DEDUCTIBLE PART OF SE TAX	16,227.	17,360.	1,133.
TOTAL ADJUSTMENTS	16,227.	17,360.	1,133.
ADJUSTED GROSS INCOME	-58,282.	684,083.	742,365.
MEDICAL AND DENTAL EXPENSES	17,118.	0.	-17,118.
TAXES	26,231.	29,933.	3,702.
INTEREST (DEDUCTIBLE)	28,259.	27,817.	-442.
CONTRIBUTIONS	0.	181,120.	181,120.
JOB EXPENSES AND 2% MISC. DEDUCT.	30,761.	8,992.	21,769.
DISALLOWED DUE TO AGI LIMITATION	0.	-12,896.	-12,896.
TOTAL ITEMIZED DEDUCTIONS	102,369.	234,966.	132,597.
INCOME BEFORE EXEMPTIONS	-160,651.	449,117.	609,768.
PERSONAL EXEMPTIONS	3,900.	0.	-3,900.
TAXABLE INCOME	0.	449,117.	449,117.
TAX	0.	131,227.	131,227.
TAX BEFORE CREDITS	0.	131,227.	131,227.
FORM 1116 (FOREIGN TAX CREDIT)	0.	1,667.	1,667.
FORM 8801 (PRIOR YEAR MIN. TAX CR.)	0.	1.	1.
TAX AFTER NON-REFUNDABLE CREDITS	0.	129,559.	129,559.
SCHEDULE SE (SELF-EMPLOYMENT TAX)	32,453.	34,720.	2,267.
FORM 8959 (ADDITIONAL MEDICARE TAX)	3,896.	4,473.	577.
FORM 8960 (NET INVEST. INCOME TAX)	0.	319.	319.
TOTAL TAX	36,349.	169,071.	132,722.
FEDERAL INCOME TAX WITHHELD	148,166.	150,628.	2,462.
TOTAL PAYMENTS	148,166.	150,628.	2,462.
TAX OVERPAID	111,817.	0.	-111,817.
AMOUNT REFUNDED	111,817.	0.	-111,817.
BALANCE DUE	0.	18,443.	18,443.

Rather an excessive salary for preaching two sermons a week. Wonder how much it has increased over the years?

Along with the miracle-selling, Paula has carved out quite an extravagant lifestyle for herself, with the over one-million-dollar mansion and the many other benefits that she enjoys for now anyway.

Paula's son, Brad, in a recent Pastor Appreciation Day service, said Paula White "changed the world" as she served in the Trump White House.

He boasted that Paula was responsible for overturning *Roe v. Wade*, even though many Pro-Life organizations worked for over fifty years to do so.

Even more brazen boasting was that Paula was responsible for moving the United States Embassy to Jerusalem. Her son also claimed that Paula extended the life of America, and she was a "mother" to our nation.

And then the biggest boast of all was that Paula anointed Trump as king, pouring oil over his head in a ceremony reminiscent of ancient Israel anointing their kings, who were ordained by God.

The crowd gave her a standing ovation as she took her bows.

Will Paula fall again and be judged so the Lord can save her?

History has a way of repeating itself.

Video of boasting -

https://youtu.be/8MtW7BMkyDQ

Proverbs 11:18

"The wicked worketh a deceitful work: but to him, that soweth righteousness *shall be* a sure reward."

Made in United States
Orlando, FL
24 August 2023